Victorian ceramic tiles

VICTORIAN CERAMIC TILES

Julian Barnard

CHRISTIE'S INTERNATIONAL COLLECTORS SERIES

MAYFLOWER BOOKS
NEW YORK

For Penny and Christopher

Acknowledgements

The author would like to thank the following for their assistance in preparing this book and for permission to take and reproduce photographs: The Victoria and Albert Museum, London (the library staff were particularly helpful); The Royal Institute of British Architects, London; The Stoke-on-Trent City Central Library; The City Museum and Art Gallery, Stoke-on-Trent (director: Mr Arnold Mountford, Mr Kelly and their staff); The Smithsonian Institution, United States National Museum; Cincinnati Art Museum, Ohio; The Tile Council of America; The British Ceramic Tile Council; The Ironbridge Gorge Museum Trust (chairman: Mr E. Bruce Ball); The Board of Governors, St Thomas's Hospital, London; Lloyds Bank; Minton Ltd, Stoke-on-Trent; Sotheby and Co., London.

My particular thanks are due to Mr David Malkin and H. & R. Johnson-Richards Tiles Ltd, Stoke-on-Trent, to whom I am deeply indebted.

I should also like to express my personal gratitude to those who have helped in many different ways: Miss Elizabeth Aslin; Mr and Mrs P. N. Barnard; David Battie; Tony Brindley, Brian and Michael; T. H. Broad; Miss Anne Campbell; Christopher Campbell; Robert Copeland; Ian Craig; Richard Dennis; Desmond Eyles; Tony Herbert; Erica Hunningher; Stanley Johnson; Ron Leake; Laurence Loh; members of the Neatby family; Mr and Mrs David Malkin; F. H. Maw; Thomas Stevens; George Wenger; Robin Wright.

Dollar and sterling equivalents in brackets in the text are approximate and based on the exchange rate of £1 = $2.

Copyright C. 1972, 1979   by Julian Barnard

All rights reserved under International and Pan American Copyright Convention. Published in the United States by Mayflower Books Inc., 575 Lexington Avenue, New York City 10022. Originally published in England by Studio Vista, a division of Cassell Ltd, 35 Red Lion Square, London WC1R 4SG

Library of Congress Cataloging in Publication Data
Barnard, Julian.
   Victorian ceramic tiles.
(Christie's International collectors series)
   Bibliography: p.179
   Includes index.
   1. Tiles, Victorian — Great Britain. 2. Tiles, Victorian — United States. I. Title. II. Series.
NK4670.7.G7B37 1979   738.6'0942   79-17078
ISBN: 0-8317-9168-3

MANUFACTURED IN the United Kingdom
FIRST AMERICAN EDITION 1972 by New York Graphic
Reprinted 1979

Printed in Hong Kong by Colorcraft Ltd

Contents

Preface

Since the first publication of this book in 1972, the interest in Victorian tiles has increased very considerably. Not only are there many more collectors, but several museums have now recognized tiles as an important subject in their own right, not merely a curiosity. At the Gladstone Museum in Stoke-on-Trent, Staffordshire, a fine collection is permanently displayed and a major exhibition of tiles was mounted by the Wolverhampton Museum. The Ironbridge Gorge Museum in Salop is reconstructing a Victorian tile workshop and has an extensive collection of old tiles made by local firms. The Victoria and Albert Museum, London, has re-opened the Old Grill Room and Restaurant, the walls of which are lined with tiles. Murals and special pieces are being rediscovered, restored and preserved. More research has brought more information on individual firms and designers, which adds considerably to the interest for specialists. This book, however, remains a comprehensive introduction to the subject and it has not been felt necessary to make many corrections. The most significant change has been the re-assessment of the cost and value of tiles.

1 Introduction

In the last decades of the nineteenth century, ceramic tiles became so popular and their use so widespread that no household was complete without them. They were applied as architectural decoration in every possible way, in churches, hospitals, town halls, offices and shops, as well as in the smallest homes. Some of them were hand-painted or made to a commissioned design, but the vast majority were mass-produced by the big industrial potters like Minton's and Maw's. The manufacture of ceramic tiles in the nineteenth century represented an early attempt to provide mass-produced decoration for the popular market: an art form that was available to everybody. As a purely decorative surface, tiles were more widely used than almost any other material. To the historian, tiles are an important adjunct to the changing styles in Victorian architecture—from the encaustic floor tiles of the neo-Gothic buildings in the fifties and sixties, right through to the use of decorative wall tiles in the large schemes of suburban architecture at the end of the century. With the present revival of interest in nineteenth-century art and design, these decorated ceramic tiles are receiving renewed attention. But the fashion for Victoriana also reawakens the traditional debate on the nature of beauty and the nineteenth-century conflict between art and the machine. The history of Victorian tiles offers an interesting opportunity to see how this conflict arose and was, to some extent, resolved.

The history of tile making goes back at least as far as the fourth millennium BC to the decorative ceramics of the ancient Near East civilizations. In Europe tiles were not in general use until the second half of the twelfth century AD when the monastic potters started to make encaustic tiles for the floors of cathedrals and churches. Finely decorated wall tiles made in Persia and Turkey date from about the same time and for about 500 years the Arab countries produced magnificent murals with brightly coloured glazes. The Dutch tiles of the seventeenth century are well known and the English Delft of the following century have received their share of recognition. But, with the exception of a few craft potters like William De Morgan, from 1830 onwards the gentle art of tile making was dead—or so one might be led to believe. In that year, Samuel Wright was granted a patent for the manufacture of ornamental tiles by mechanical means and the modern industry was born. Although more tiles were made, for more varied purposes, than ever before, it has been a prevalent belief that tile making had slipped from grace and was no longer what William Morris called one of 'the lesser arts of life'.

William Morris's part in the reformation of mid-Victorian design ideas and his assertion of a conscious craft tradition is well documented. Following the lead of men like Ruskin, Morris sought to re-establish the ethics of art and design and this was to involve a rejection of the machine and the products of the Industrial Revolution. But how far did Morris go towards solving the growing demands of a consumer society in an industrial age? By following the development of one particular industry, it can be seen how manufacturers responded to the changing climate of public taste and popular demand. The history of Victorian tiles is typical of a far wider field of 'art industries' that have been largely neglected. There has been a tendency among nineteenth-century art historians to pay exclusive attention to the work of a few leading figures of the period and to ignore the mainstream of activity. Except for a small number of connoisseurs, it is in the market-place that most people do their shopping.

Although there was no outcry about the mass-production of functional articles like drainpipes and roofing tiles, when the machine entered the sacred precincts of Art, then there were only two possible courses of action (and during the last hundred years both of them have been followed). It was necessary either to redefine the meaning of the subject and embrace the full implications of the machine, or to establish a reactionary movement that would attempt to counteract the Industrial Revolution and rebuild the sacred temple of man's aspiration to individual expression of Beauty and Art. In the event the Victorians chose the latter course. The decision was made easier by the evident destruction of human values that the machine might bring. But it was a mistake to think that the machine was to blame, rather than the social system. For although capitalism was responsible for the exploitation of labour it was also responsible for the growth of the consumer market that industry was to serve. And once this relationship had been established, it was virtually impossible to break it. There was a clear correlation between the newly emergent middle class and the expansion of those industries producing semi-functional and decorative products. That a large proportion of these goods were badly designed and ill-conceived is beyond dispute.

The early Victorian reformers, like Henry Cole and A. Welby Pugin, were less concerned with the evils of the machine and more intent on combating the lack of taste shown by most designers and the ignorance of the true principles of architecture and ornament. For Pugin the subject was closely coupled with his Catholic faith and belief in the nobility of the ecclesiastical architecture of the Middle Ages. The return to medievalism in decoration was an essential aspect of the work of men like Pugin and Morris. It was generally held that English architecture had mistakenly followed continental fashions and as a result had completely lost any sense of national identity. In order to combat the eclecticism of the 1830s and 1840s, many architects looked back 400 years to the flowering of the Gothic style and drew freely upon that period as a source-book or grammar of ornament. The rebirth of the encaustic tile coincided with the Gothic revival in English architecture and was an important stage-prop of the movement. Encaustic tiles were used extensively in almost every big building, both secular and ecclesiastical, that was built or restored in the second half of the century. As one writer observed: 'and soon no ecclesiastical building having any pretentions to architectural superiority, will be considered complete in its decoration without them.'[1] In cooperation with Herbert Minton, Pugin was instrumental in laying the foundations of this market for encaustic tiles. During the early years these floor tiles were essentially medieval in character and blended perfectly with Pugin's work as a Church architect. His belief in simple and authentic ornament did not preclude the use of the machine.

It was Ruskin who was to herald the Craft Revival, with his lectures and writings on art, during the middle decades of the century. Ruskin inspired Morris in his ideals of the total reform that was needed to counteract not just the decline of the decorative arts but the evils of a capitalist industrial society.

The nineteenth century was a great age of expansion for Britain, both at home and in the colonies. All kinds of commercial enterprise brought a new affluence to many people and this was paralleled by an increasing demand for every kind of product, not least those that fall under the heading of the 'decorative arts'. As these new markets developed, so the manufacturers were able to increase production. The pottery industry, from the late eighteenth century onwards, took advantage of any mechanical inventions that might lend themselves to economies in time and labour to enable the supply to keep up with demand. A typical example (apart from the use of the steam engine) was the introduction of 'jigger' and 'jolly' machines which assisted in the throwing and pressing of plates and bowls.* As far as tiles were concerned, this move to mass-production was particularly evident in the nineteenth century and a succession of patents were taken out during the first decades of Victoria's reign in order to manufacture the object in large enough quantities (the quality was less crucial) to satisfy the ever increasing demands of a consumer society. By 1873, an article in *The Builder* remarked:

> As we have pointed out once or twice already, when touching on the subject, the use of ornamental polychrome decoration is being carried to an indiscriminate and disproportionate extent, so much as to be degenerating into a mere piece of commonplace . . . the difficulty is, often, to find anything that does not have a tile in it.[2]

The complaint was not about the poor quality of the design, but the fact that tiles were so common. The truth is that the arbiters of good taste could never really reconcile themselves to the facts of industrial production. If something was good, then how did it stop being good by overuse? The answer lies, to some extent, in the question of what was appropriate decoration. As always, Morris had something to say on the subject:

* It is interesting that trades union opposition to these machines, led by William Evans in the 1830s, delayed their effective use for many years.

As to the surface decoration on pottery, it is clear it must never be printed . . . one rule we have for a guide and whatever we do if we abide by it, we are sure to go wrong if we neglect it: and it is common to all the lesser arts. Think of your material. Don't paint anything on pottery save what can only be painted on pottery; if you do it is clear that however good a draughtsman you may be, you do not care about that special art.[3]

The idea of 'that special art' was important to Morris—a true craftsman should be passionate about his subject and every part of his production should be an expression of that particular medium. Clay for the potter, wool for the weaver. And as a man understood his material, so he could use pattern and decoration in a way that was naturally suitable. For this reason, printed decoration could never be considered 'artistic'.

Through the agency of Morris and his contemporaries, the public became more aware of 'Art' and 'Beauty' than ever before. The harlequinade of early Victorian decoration turned into a conscious striving for good taste in design and ornament that found many disparate (and desperate) expressions in the Art or Aesthetic Movement during the last quarter of the century. But the public contemplation of the nature of what was 'truly artistic' led to fashions, in the seventies and eighties, that were far removed from the original intentions of the Art Movement. Morris had looked for a revival of craft and cottage industry, but the industrial manufacturers responded, not by changing their production techniques, but by advertising their wares as 'art furniture': there were 'celebrated and artistic' billiard tables, 'more truly artistic' textiles, 'art metal workers'; but more than anything else, there were 'art tiles'.

The popular pursuit of Beauty and Art was, in fact, the one thing that saved the industrial manufacturers from embarrassment. There was nothing so certain to guarantee the future of mass-production as fashion. Oscar Wilde, drawing on the ideas of Ruskin and Morris, was one of the men who ensured the success of the Art Movement:

[Although] Beauty had existed long before 1880, it was Mr Oscar Wilde who managed her début. To study the period is to admit that to him was due no small part of the social vogue that Beauty began to enjoy. Fired by his fervid words, men and women hurled their mahogany into the streets and ransacked the curio shops for furniture of Annish days. Dados [of tiles] arose on every wall, sunflowers and the feathers of peacocks curled in every corner, tea grew cold while guests were praising the Willow Pattern of its cups.[4]

The Aesthetic Movement points to the gulf that existed between the general public and the contemporary intellectuals, such as the exponents of the Arts and Crafts Tradition. The popular response to the reforms in art and design was superficial. It was decoration that was fashionable and there was little concern for the object or how it was made. If some pundits were lamenting the fruits of the machine age, most people were revelling in the novelty and variety of goods that could be purchased. Towards the end of the century there was some reconciliation between these two positions. Although Morris always held firmly to his socialist views, he did come to recognize the necessity of the machine. And at the same time there had been a general improvement in the standards of the commercial manufacturers. The work of men like Ashbee and Lethaby was to bring the products of the Arts and Crafts Movement to a far wider public and the prevalent outlook was explained by a member of the Boston Arts and Crafts Society, United States: 'There is an antagonism between business for the sake of gain and Art for the sake of use and beauty, but the antagonism is between their motives, not between business and art.'[5]

Although the motives of the commercial potters were questionable, tile production came into the category of 'business for the sake of use and beauty'. But the essential characteristic of the industry was mechanical production. The same writer goes on to remark that 'it is wholesome now and then to turn suddenly round and ask ourselves, when we are thinking of the wonders of mechanical invention which the last few generations have seen, "Just whose labour does machinery save?"' The question was important to the exponents of the Craft Tradition. It is clear, however, that machinery was not designed to save labour but to increase production. Never before had tiles been used so extensively: on walls, floors, in furniture, grates and hearths. And in an age when architecture was often seen as something to stick on to a building afterwards, to make it showy, tiles were used by every speculative builder in the country. In the concentric rings of nineteenth-century development around English towns and cities, tiled pavements and porches can be seen in their thousands. They took their place with the odd pieces of stained glass in the front door, the cast-iron railings, the terracotta ridge tiles and the little panels of decorative brickwork on the façade.

2 Industrial production: Mr Minton, Mr Wright and Mr Prosser

There were three English centres of tile production in the eighteenth century—London, Bristol and Liverpool. In 1756, John Sadler (1720–89), from Liverpool, produced the first mechanically decorated tiles, using a transfer printing process that was to revolutionize the whole of the pottery industry. A contemporary affidavit, that was sent with the application for the patent, says that Sadler, with the help of Guy Green, 'without the aid or assistance of any other person or persons, did, within the space of six hours, to whit, betwixt the hours of nine in the morning and three in the afternoon of the same day, print upwards of 1200 Earthenware tiles of different patterns at Liverpoole . . . more in number and better and neater than one hundred skilful pot-painters could have painted in the like space of time.'[6] After they were fired it was generally agreed that they were more elegant than any seen before, that would have been painted by hand. It is more significant, perhaps, that they could also be sold for half the price. When Josiah Wedgwood first became acquainted with the process he was strongly critical of the idea of printing decoration. His first reaction was that a work of art must be hand-painted. But it was not long before crates of biscuit-fired pots were travelling to Liverpool from Burslem, returning with a printed pattern upon them, that had been executed by Messrs Sadler and Green for Mr Josiah Wedgwood.

This printing technique allowed a great deal of detail and subtlety in drawing. The quality of the hand-painted tiles had degenerated considerably in the attempt to produce too many too quickly. But with this new process any amount of time could be spent on the original drawing, since to decorate the actual tile would take only a few seconds. As well as the practical benefits that were attached to this invention, it also liberated eighteenth-century tile design from the traditional and overworked motifs of the old Delft tiles (plate 1). The new Liverpool designs were fresh, lively and full of interest; some 250 of them are recorded with scenes of gallantry, sport, satire and fable; two series depicted actors and actresses in their principal stage roles (plate 2). Sadler realized that if his new method of printing tiles was to be accepted, he would have to do something completely different as far as decoration was concerned. He demonstrated that printed tiles, far from being cheap imitations, were more exact, detailed and interesting than all but the very best contemporary hand-painted tiles.

The work of Sadler and Green gives an important context to the developments of the nineteenth century. They had succeeded in mass-producing the decorative element in the tile but the tile itself was still cut and shaped by hand, a laborious business that involved beating out the clay, cutting it to the required size and slowly drying it. It had to be handled several times before it was in a fit state to be fired. It was not until the tile body could be made with the same ease and speed as it was decorated that industrial production was really under way. The man effectively responsible for this development was Herbert Minton (1793–1858). With a few notable exceptions 'the history of the manufacture of encaustic and other tiles by Minton, Hollins and Co. is the history of the entire modern trade in these useful and beautiful articles.'[7]

Minton's was established in 1793 by Thomas Minton. But it was his son Herbert who was responsible for the firm's involvement in the production of tiles. Herbert Minton joined his father in the business in 1817 and the records suggest that it was in 1828 that he first became interested in reviving the lost art of making encaustic tiles. These tiles were made by a completely different process to the simple wall tiles that Sadler and Green were using. They were thicker and heavier and, instead of having a surface glaze decoration, the pattern was set into the body of the tile to a depth of about $\frac{1}{8}$ in., using a different coloured clay. The inlaid pattern was fused into the body during the firing process. The monastic potters of medieval Europe had excelled in the production of these tiles and from the twelfth to the sixteenth centuries they were used extensively for the floors of ecclesiastical buildings (plate 3). But it was a skill that had died with the Reformation and the closing of the monasteries in 1540–60. For nearly three hundred years it was forgotten, and it was not until the middle of the nineteenth century that archaeologists discovered the sites of some of the old kilns and enthusiasts began to examine and record the designs of the medieval tiles that could still be found in many cathedrals and churches. Excavation revealed more, and contemporary periodicals published several articles on Romano-British and medieval ceramic tiles.

It may have been chance that drew Herbert Minton's attention to the commercial possibilities of tile manufacture; it was a fortunate coincidence, in that case, because another man was working on the idea at the same time. Quite independently, Samuel Wright, a potter from Shelton, had been carrying out research and in 1830 he was granted a patent by the Crown for the mechanical production of encaustic tiles. Wright made some attempt to manufacture by means of this process but did not meet with any commercial success. After his initial enthusiasm, Minton had found other work too pressing to allow a full investigation into the matter—he eagerly bought a share in the patent and began to develop and perfect the technique. Wright retained an interest and held a ten per cent royalty on all the tiles sold during the fourteen years that the patent lasted.

These tiles were made with a plastic clay body; the shape of the pattern was impressed using a plaster mould and the indented area was filled with a different coloured clay, in slip form. The patent reads:

A manufacture of ornamental tiles, bricks and quarries for floors, pavements and other purposes. First making these articles of fine clays, and firing them until semi-vitrified. Second ornamenting them in various colours and with various patterns similar to the patterns on a carpet etc, by impressing them with the patterns and filling up the impressions with clay etc, coloured with metal oxides. The patterns are impressed by moulding them in moulds of plaster of paris in metal frames. The articles are reduced to the same size thickness by a cutting instrument worked upon a machine, which keeps the article at a true level.[8]

There were considerable technical difficulties, particularly in the firing of the tile. Jewitt, in *The Ceramic Art of Great Britain* (1878), says:

Mr Minton commenced the manufacture in a single room . . . at the earthenware works, and only three men were at first employed. He was much aided in his task by the late Mr George Leason, a practical potter, who had been brought up under him. . . . Difficulties had to be encountered, chiefly arising from the irregular contraction of the clays. Sometimes the inlaid parts would, at a slight tap at the back of the tile, fall out, or the tiles would become stained in firing; and in short all sorts of ill luck and misadventures were the weekly result. The tiles were at first fired in a small oven at the china works which would hold about 700 tiles and he and his fellow labourers used regularly to go there to witness the drawing of the oven. Time after time they found nearly the whole contents spoilt in one way or other, and they were carted away to form part of the foundation on which many of our pottery streets now stand. If it so happened that 100 out of the 700 proved fairly good, the fact was a source of encouragement to all concerned. Repeated failures, however, were only followed by further experiments. Mr Minton was ever confident that skill and perseverance would in the end prove a success; but surely never was any man's patience or pocket more sorely or severely tried.[9]

It was several years before the results were reliable and the product good enough to be marketed. The Stoke City Library has a catalogue marked 'the earliest pattern book of the first encaustic tiles made in England by Herbert Minton in 1835'. Sixty-two designs are illustrated. In April 1836 Minton sent Josiah Booker, of Liverpool, a plan for tiling the hall-floor of his house. The design was accepted. At the end of the year Minton wrote the following letter to a Mr Monat of Lerwick, Shetlands, though it is not known what became of the matter:

> Stoke on Trent 27th Dec. 1836
> Staffordshire Potteries
>
> Sir,
> Having purchased the patent for making tepilated [sic] pavements from Mr Wright, he has handed me your letter of the 8th inst. and agreeable to your request I now send you sketches of the pavement,

which are composed of a buff ground with black ornaments, the price of which is 18/- pr, square yard, or six [pence] each six inch square tile. The four first drawings are for bo . . . [borders?] and the remainder for the . . . [central section?] but if you have any particular design fit for general use that you wish to have executed, I will gladly make models and moulds free of any expense to you but if you . . . I shall have to charge you for the models and moulds. If you would like to see specimens of the tiles I will send 2 or 3 to y'r Liverpool agents upon hearing from you to that effect. The above price is subject to an additional charge for packing and exclusive of the usual freight to Liverpool which is about 12/6 from Stoke.

I am Sir y'r ob. serv't

Herbert Minton.[10]

A year later another commission was obtained for a decorated pavement in the mansion at Kilmoray, belonging to Sir John P. Orde, Bart. But most of the experimental tiles made in the early years were given away to friends, and Samuel Wright probably earned very little money from his ten per cent royalty. Minton was not worried by the lack of commercial success; he was quite content to invest in the future. He was determined to reproduce the medieval examples to the same quality and standard. At times he had to face great disappointment and criticism. but he was determined to succeed. When Boyle, a partner in the firm from 1836–41, suggested the project should be abandoned, Minton's reply was characteristic: 'Say no more on the subject Mr Boyle, I will make these tiles if they cost me a guinea each.'

Wright's patent ran until 1844 when it was bought in equal shares by Minton's and Chamberlain's of Worcester. The Worcester firm, under the name of Fleming St John, G. Barr, had held an interest in the process for some time. They were moderately successful in manufacturing encaustic tiles. In 1844 an advertisement appeared in the *Gentleman's Magazine* offering a catalogue with seventy-seven designs for tile pavements. But the fortunes of the firm were varied and in the end the tile stock was sold to John Hornby Maw (1800–85), a retired businessman, who had made his fortune as a manufacturing chemist, making baby bottles. Maw lived in Brighton in a house next door to the artist William Turner, and having retired at the modest age of thirty-four was looking for a hobby—by the 1890s Maw's had become the largest tile manufacturers in the world. In the early years, however, it was Herbert Minton who was responsible for the pioneering work and it is hardly surprising that when a new technique for producing ceramics was invented he was first in the queue to buy a share in it. One particular process, invented by Richard Prosser, from Birmingham, and patented 17 June 1840, was for making clay buttons. But with considerable acumen, Minton saw that the process had far greater potential. Prosser had developed a method of making buttons from dry or dust clay. The idea was simple: the clay was compressed between two metal dies. The object was perfectly formed and ready for firing in a couple of seconds. Minton immediately bought a share in the patent, realizing that if the process worked for making buttons it could also be used for tiles.

Production at Stoke began two months later, in August 1840. In a letter to Jewitt, Mr Turley, the chief engineer at Minton's, recalled that they started with seven presses: one large press for making tiles, and six smaller presses forming buttons and tesserae for mosaic floors. By September 1842, altogether sixty-two presses were in operation and 'the demand for white glazed tiles was soon very great'. At this stage the presses were not used for making encaustic tiles but for wall tiles, which could now be mass-produced for the first time. The ingenuity of the method aroused considerable interest and on 8 March 1843 the process was exhibited at the Society of Arts, London. Three days later:

> The same press and process was exhibited by Mr Turley at the Marquess of Northampton's soirée as President of the British Association—a brilliant gathering, at which were present Prince Albert, the Duke of Wellington, Sir Robert Peel, a number of Bishops and about thirty foreign Princes. The late Prince Consort took so much interest in the process that Mr Prosser and Mr Minton decided that a description of the process and a drawing of the press, as then seen at work, should be prepared forthwith and presented to his Highness, which was done and presented 15th March 1843.[11]

It must have been an exciting time for Minton. Apart from the success of the new technique for making wall tiles, the long years of research that had been invested in encaustic tiles were beginning to bear fruit. In 1841, the firm executed their first important job—the floor of Temple Church in London. Minton had copied the designs from the Chapter House at Westminster Abbey (1253–59) and clearly felt that the modern tiles were satisfactory imitations of the originals. A catalogue of 1842 illustrated a wide variety of patterns, most of which were direct copies of medieval designs with heraldic devices or groups of saints (plate 5). At this date the encaustic tiles were made in a limited range of colours because of the problems posed by differential contraction of different coloured clays. A red clay body with a white figure (the traditional colours of the originals) presented the fewest difficulties and was most commonly used, although black and buff tiles were also made.

The success that Minton and Prosser enjoyed when demonstrating the new patent tile press to the Society of Arts and to the British Association drew attention to Minton's encaustic tiles; the following year, in 1844, a decorated pavement was made for Osborne House, Queen Victoria's residence on the Isle of Wight. It was the first of many commissions executed for the Royal Family. The 'thirty foreign Princes' soon swelled the ranks of customers too. In fact the guest-list at the soirée gives an interesting indication of the early tiling jobs carried out by Minton's. Sir Robert Peel, Prime Minister at that time, died before

1 Bristol Delftware tiles, mid-eighteenth century; hand-painted polychrome designs with traditional images. Victoria & Albert Museum, London.

2 Sadler & Green, printed tiles, *c.* 1770; Sadler's patent of 1756 represented the first attempt at mass-production with a printed pattern. The lively scenes of eighteenth-century English life were a refreshing change from the overworked motifs of the Delft tiles. Victoria & Albert Museum, London.

3 Medieval encaustic tile from Keynsham Abbey, late-thirteenth century; 5. in. red body with a white pattern inlaid. Victoria & Albert Museum, London.

4 Minton & Co., *c.* 1845; 5 in. encaustic tile copied from a medieval design. The same tile is illustrated in an early catalogue (plate 5). By permission City Museum, Stoke-on-Trent.

5 Page from Minton & Co.'s catalogue, entitled 'Old English Tile Design', 1842. Most of the patterns imitated medieval encaustic tiles, others were non-figurative with geometrical patterns. By permission Victoria & Albert Museum, London.

6 Victorian encaustic tiles, 6 in.: *top left*: Minton & Co., *c.* 1870; blue, brown, red and buff, unglazed. *top right*: Minton & Co., *c.* 1880; black, white and buff, glazed. *middle left*: no marks, *c.* 1870; dust-pressed encaustic tile, black and grey, unglazed. The simplicity of the two-colour design was particularly suited to this process. *middle right*: Maw & Co., *c.* 1885; white and buff, glazed. *bottom left*: Minton & Co., *c.* 1880; brown, blue, white and buff, glazed. *bottom right*: Minton & Co., *c.* 1865; yellow and blue, unglazed.

7 J. C. Edwards, Victorian Jubilee tile; brown body with a white slip pattern drawn through a stencil.

8 Campbell Brick & Tile Co., *c.* 1880; browns, buff, blues and red, 12 in. An elaborate six-colour encaustic tile. By permission City Museum, Stoke-on-Trent.

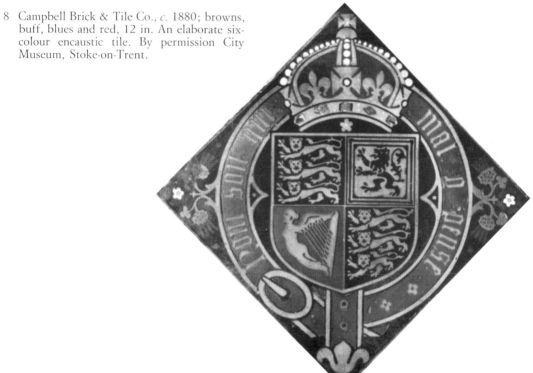

9 Minton, Hollins & Co., *c*. 1850; an early litho-printed tile made under the Collins & Reynolds patent, blue, buff, green and plum with white body, 12 in. By permission City Museum, Stoke-on-Trent.

10 Minton's China Works, 1877; sgraffito panel designed by M. L. Solon, 13 in. The brown body was coated with white slip and the pattern reversed out by scraping away the clay to reveal the colour beneath. One of a pair of tiles depicting the gentle art of the potter. By permission City Museum, Stoke-on-Trent.

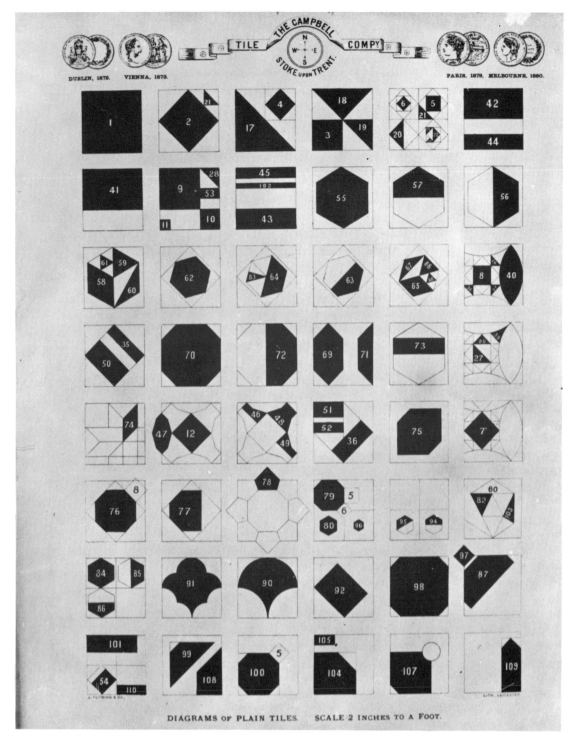

11 Page from Campbell's catalogue, 1885, illustrating the shaped tiles available for geometric pavements. Each pattern was made in a range of colours which allowed considerable freedom for designs. By permission Victoria & Albert Museum, London.

12

13

14

15

12 Leon Arnoux (1816-1902) joined Minton's in 1849 and was Art Director of the company for many years. He was responsible for several of the developments in glazing and decorating techniques. By permission Victoria & Albert Museum, London.

13 Samuel Keyes, superintendant of the Pittsburgh Encaustic Tile Co., was one of the first Americans to make encaustic tiles successfully, in 1867. By permission Victoria & Albert Museum, London.

14 Herbert Minton (1793-1858), more than any other man, was responsible for the growth of the Victorian tile industry. By permission Victoria & Albert Museum, London.

15 Joseph Edge of Malkin, Edge & Co.; taken from a photograph album 'Presented to Joseph Edge Esq. on his attaining his 80th birthday by the employees of the Newport Tile and Earthenware Works as a token of their respect and high esteem for his benevolent character and invariable kindliness 14 July 1885.' Collection H. & R. Johnson - Richards.

16

16 Tiles provided the best kind of panel decoration in furniture since the designs were permanent. The use of tiles in this way owed something to the panel paintings by Morris and Burne-Jones in the late 1850s. The eight-inch tile used here is a red transfer-printed design on a buff ground by Minton's China Works, *c.* 1880. It is one of a set of twelve, designed by J. Moyr Smith, illustrating Scott's *Waverley* novels. Victoria & Albert Museum, London.

17 Cabinet with tile inserts made by Doulton & Co., displayed at the International Exhibition, 1872. The designs, by Hannah Barlow, were incised into the slip-coated plastic clay. Victoria & Albert Museum, London.

17

18 Fireplace by Maw & Co., *c.* 1870, cast in Majolica Ware. One of a set of three taken from the old offices of the company in Jackfield; it is now displayed in the fireplace showrooms of H. & R. Johnson-Richards, Stoke-on-Trent. Collection H. & R. Johnson-Richards.

19 Victorian fireplace and surround, *c.* 1890, in an office entrance, Maddox Street, London. The dado of tiles is typical of those in many public buildings. The grate is on casters to facilitate cleaning.

GLEDHOW HALL. LEEDS.

J. Kitson Jun.ᵣ Esqᵣ

BATH-ROOM in BURMANTOFT FAIENCE.

Mess.ʳˢ Chorley and Connon.
Architects.

20 Tiled bathroom by Burmantoft's, 1885. By permission Victoria and Albert Museum, London.

21 Drawings from Maw's catalogue, 1883, showing possible uses for tiles in an entrance hall, a railway station and a public house. By permission Victoria & Albert Museum, London.

22 Maw & Co's stand at the Chicago Exhibition, 1893. This display was so well received in America that it was kept by the Columbian Museum, Chicago. It cost £300 [$720] to build, but was not exceptionally elaborate by contemporary standards. By permission Victoria and Albert Museum, London.

23 Drawings for a tiled fireplace by William De Morgan, *c.* 1890; designed for Lord Ashburton's yacht — ships and fishes were some of De Morgan's favourite tile subjects. By permission Victoria & Albert Museum, London.

24 Sketch for fireplace tiles, 1883, by George C. Haité (1855-1924), for Burmantoft's of Leeds. By permission Victoria & Albert Museum, London.

25 A selection of medals won by Maw & Co. at international exhibitions, including Dublin 1872, Paris 1875, 1889, Sydney 1879 and Barcelona 1888. Collection H. & R. Johnson-Richards.

26 Letters Patent granted to Herbert Minton and James Nasmyth, 1856. Nasmyth was a distinguished engineer and this patent probably related to some modification in machinery used at Minton's. Collection H. & R. Johnson-Richards.

27 Page from Maw & Co's catalogue, 1883, illustrating a selection of majolica tiles. With clear layouts and good quality printing, catalogues were the most effective means of selling tiles. By permission Victoria & Albert Museum, London.

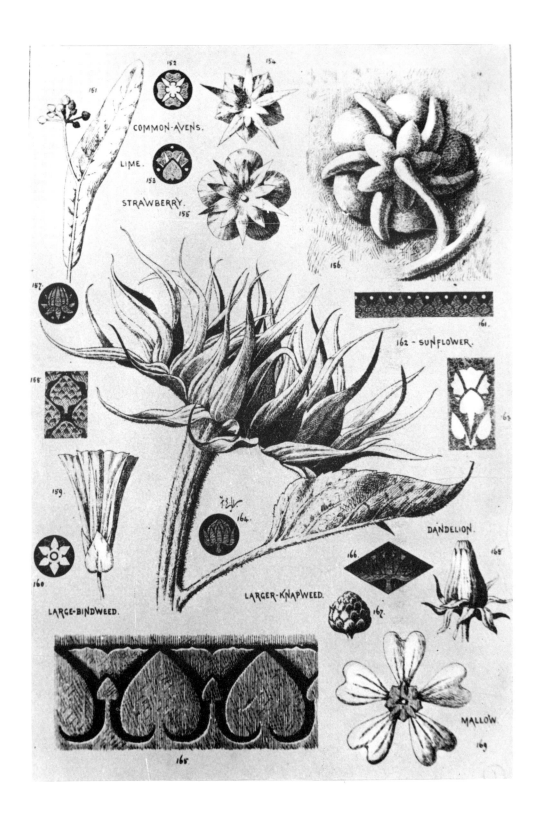

151

152 COMMON-AVENS.
154

LIME.
153

STRAWBERRY.
155

156.

157

158

161

162 - SUNFLOWER.

163

159

164

DANDELION.

160

166

168

LARGE-BINDWEED.

LARGER-KNAPWEED.

167

165

MALLOW.

169

28 Design sheet by F. E. Hulme FSA, typical of the studies abstracting decorative motifs from natural forms, 1870. Many tile patterns were devised in this way. By permission Victoria & Albert Museum, London.

the new Houses of Parliament were completed in 1852, so he was not destined to walk in the corridors at Westminster that were paved with Minton tiles. The Bishops were very important spectators: the Church was to become Minton's largest single customer.* Among the early 'restoration' jobs done with encaustic tiles were the cathedrals at Ely, Gloucester and Salisbury. One of the first schemes in America was for the new Capitol Buildings in Washington (1855), where an extensive encaustic tile floor was made for the House of Representatives.

By 1858, when Herbert Minton died, encaustic tiles were in general use. By way of an obituary, the Lichfield Diocesan Church Calendar of 1859 listed well over 150 churches paved with his tiles. He had made a gift to the cathedral of a pavement for the chancel and this in their opinion was the best memorial to their benefactor. The future of the business had been well established: in 1845, Mrs Minton's nephew, Michael Daintry Hollins (?–1898), had been taken into partnership and, a year later, Samuel Wright's son had also joined the firm. Another nephew, Colin Minton Campbell (1827–85), joined in 1849. Wright had continued his father's work and in 1855 a new patent was taken out (see page 48) for the manufacture of encaustic tiles. The determination that carried through the early years of failure and disappointment, now manifested itself in constant discoveries about the possibilities for decorating tiles. Monsieur Leon Arnoux (1816–1902), Art Director at Minton's for many years, pioneered the discovery of glazing techniques in imitation of the old Moorish and Italian tiles. By 1850 Minton's had introduced a new series of opaque enamels that they called 'majolica ware'. At the Great Exhibition of 1851 their tiles graced the Alhambra Court at the Crystal Palace. In the same year a new technique for transfer printing tiles had been successfully developed under a patent held by Minton's in conjunction with Messrs Collins and Reynolds (plate 9). Some of the first tiles of this sort were used by Pugin to decorate the walls of the smoking room in the House of Commons.

It was some time before Minton's supremacy was challenged. Other firms, however, had already begun to manufacture tiles. Fleming St John, G. Barr & Co. of Worcester had amalgamated in 1840 with their local rivals, Chamberlain's. In 1848, they stopped making tiles, but the remaining stock was bought by Maw & Co. in 1850. Finding that the clay in Worcester was unsatisfactory, they moved, two years later, to the Benthall Works near Broseley, Shropshire. At first the company

* The front page of Minton Hollins's catalogue of 1881 gave a full list of the prestige jobs that had been undertaken:
The following are some of the places in which tiling has been carried out by Messrs Minton Hollins & Co.:—The Royal Palaces of Windsor, Osborne, Clarence House, Sandringham and Marlborough House; the Imperial Palace of the Emperor of Germany; the Palace and State Yachts of the Sultan of Turkey; the Royal Residence of Prince Dhuleep Singh; the Houses of Parliament, Westminster; the New Foreign Offices; the New Government Buildings in India and Australia; the South Kensington Museum; the Albert Hall; the Senior and Junior Carlton Clubs; the Cathedrals of Ely, Lincoln, Lichfield, Gloucester, Westminster, Wells, Glasgow, Armagh, St Giles' Edinburgh, Dunblane and Sydney (New South Wales); The New Capitol of Washington (US of America); the Town Halls of Liverpool, Leeds, Rochdale, Bolton, etc.; the Municipal Buildings of Birmingham and Liverpool; and many of the principal Ducal Mansions, Government Buildings, Churches and Public Institutions of Great Britain, etc.

barely paid its expenses and full commercial production did not begin until about 1857. Another early contender was the firm of Copeland and Garrett; Jewitt records that they started making encaustic tiles in 1836 and that they were one of the earliest firms to be successful. Although dates are often uncertain, there were a few other firms operating before Minton's death. The Architectural Pottery of Poole was established in 1854 and Messrs T. & R. Boote bought the Waterloo Works in 1850. Boote's later became one of the best known tile manufacturers and were the first to make encaustic tiles from clay dust, using a technique that was invented by Boulton and Worthington in 1863 (see page 48).

But Herbert Minton was the acknowledged master of tile making during the first half of the nineteenth century: 'The late Welby Pugin, the eminent Gothic architect, was heard frequently to remark that, if Mr Minton had done nothing more for his country than the revival of this beautiful art, there ought to be a public statue erected to his memory, with one hand holding a specimen of his tiles.'[12] It was said that his encaustic tiles were the greatest step ever made in architectural decoration by the English ceramics industry.

Pugin (1812–52), the pioneer of the Gothic Revival, was an intimate friend of Herbert Minton's. Writing in 1861, Benjamin Ferrey says that 'among the various objects occupying Pugin's attention, not one received a greater share than the revival of encaustic tiles.'[13] Pugin and Minton had a close and sometimes stormy relationship and in the last years of his life it appears that Pugin quarrelled violently over the design of the tiles for Westminster. Overwork had upset his health, mentally and physically, and he wrote emotional letters to Minton from his sick-bed. But a reconciliation was effected by Pugin's wife, and in January 1852 he wrote to Herbert saying: 'I declare your St Stephen's tiles the finest done in the tile way; vastly superior to any ancient work; in fact they are the best tiles in the world, and I think my patterns and your workmanship go ahead of anything.'[14] Most of Pugin's buildings made use of tiles. His enthusiasm gave great impetus to Minton's business and undoubtedly his adoption of encaustic tiles for ecclesiastical building established their use for the rest of the century.

The expanse of a church floor was ideal for encaustic tiles. Pavements could be made up in any number of ways to give emphasis to nave and sanctuary. And the architect employed would often design his own scheme, selecting the tiles from a catalogue and then specifying a layout. In the early years each tile was a complete unit in its own right. But as expertise increased, the range of possibilities became almost infinite. By 1880, up to six colours could be used in one tile to form a pattern that might be made up from several hundred units. As a general principle it is possible to judge the date of an encaustic tile from the complexity of the pattern and the number of colours used (plate 6). As a very general guide, red tiles with a white figure are the earliest, then browns and buffs; blue tiles with a yellow/buff figure were popular in the sixties and were followed by more subtle colour schemes using a strong chocolate red with a quiet grey. Glazed encaustic tiles, often with a clean white body and a black or gold design, were used towards the end of the century and in the same period they were made with complicated patterns involving white, black, gold, pinks, greens and blues. Perhaps the best work was done in the early seventies when Maw's were commissioning designs from men like M. Digby Wyatt, George Goldie, J. P. Seddon and George Street. Some of the designs were original, though many were taken from Roman and medieval examples. Fine pavements from this period can still be seen today in many churches and cathedrals in Great Britain.

The popularity of encaustic tiles and their use in public buildings proliferated and in a modified form they were used extensively in domestic architecture. But the scale of the design was often so small in hallways and corridors that figured encaustic tiles were not really suitable and expense stood in the way of their more general use. For this reason a different type of tile pavement known as 'geometric' had been introduced at an early date. These tiles were geometrical segments from a six-inch square (plate 11) that were made individually, in a range of colours. Different patterns could be made up, using various shapes and sizes. Since each piece involved only one colour, it could be stamped from dust clay using Prosser's patent and geometric tiles were certainly manufactured before the 1863 patent for making encaustic tiles by the dust process. Strictly speaking these were not encaustic tiles, although that name is often used to describe them. Geometric and encaustic tiles were often used together on a floor. Examples can be seen in the Victoria and Albert Museum, many parish churches and in most Victorian houses throughout Great Britain.

But few encaustic tiles were used in domestic architecture after the turn of the century. By 1898, *The Builder* recorded that rubber interlocking floor tiles were being introduced into England, from America. The new rubber tiles were hard, durable, slip-proof, coloured and patterned; they were easier to handle, being much lighter and thinner; they did not break; and above all, they were easier to lay. The expense of laying a geometric floor was almost as great as the cost of the tiles themselves. Although the manufacturer could recommend the services of various 'fixers' or would supply instructions to the builder, it was not the simplest way to cover a floor. In the past there had always been difficulties with cleaning the tiles (grease spots were particularly troublesome) and there had been heated debates in the correspondence columns of *The Builder* about the reasons for a calcareous growth that afflicted several households. The problem turned out to be an efflorescence of lime and was the result of bedding the tiles in the wrong material. The new rubber tiles could simply be cut to shape by hand and glued down; they were altogether more practical, if less interesting. But people were ready for a change and encaustic tiles were about to become redundant.

3 The fashion for tiles

Minton's early success with encaustic tiles was directly attributable to his demonstration at the Marquess of Northampton's soirée in 1843. He was able to introduce his product to some of the most influential men in the country and also to a number of foreign dignitaries. There can be little doubt that this was a break-through. He had an interesting and ingenious manufacturing process, a good product and a captive audience, composed of the men who were in the best position to buy. This was one way of tackling the problem of marketing. It might be called 'prestige selling'. Nineteenth-century art critics were always keen to praise the discrimination and good taste shown by Queen Victoria and Prince Albert—if they liked tiles then a good start had been made. The sequel to this kind of promotional work was more important since it reached a far wider audience. The second half of the century was the age of the Great Exhibitions, equivalent to our World's Fairs. The exhibitions acted as a forum for every kind of product, from many different countries, offering the public an opportunity to see exactly what there was to buy. Awards were made for excellence in the different fields of manufacture and although the French ran away with most of the prizes at the first international exhibition, held at the Crystal Palace in 1851, the English designers were soon to win an international reputation. In a tile catalogue from Maw & Co. it is proudly announced that the firm had won medals in London 1862, 1874; Oporto 1865; Dublin 1865; Paris 1867, 1889; Philadelphia 1876; Melbourne 1880, 1888; and more than twenty others (plate 25). The importance of such recognition is best seen in the case of the American tile company of J. G. Low. Greatly impressed by the tiles at the Philadelphia Centennial Exhibition in 1876, Mr John Low decided to set up his own factory. After just over a year he was competing directly with English firms at an exhibition in Crewe, Cheshire, and he won the gold medal, establishing his company as one of the foremost tile producers in the world.

For those who did not actually visit these exhibitions, many of the magazines and journals of the period made full reports with descriptions of this or that firm's tiles, with prices and a few remarks as to the design and quality of the product. The great increase in the number of periodicals published during the seventies and eighties was a result of the popular interest in design and decoration which was fostered by the Art Movement. Magazines like *The Builder* had been enthusiastic about tile production for many years. But more ephemeral publications such as *The Decorator and Furnisher* (New York 1882–98) brought the gospel of aestheticism to the public and were an important vehicle for advertising 'art tiles'. Many periodicals carried a short paragraph about a new catalogue or a set of sample tiles that the editor had received, and his remarks, if they were complimentary, were good publicity for the manufacturer. More lengthy reviews on the developments of the tile industry brought tiles to the public's attention and one magazine often followed the fortunes of a particular firm or designer and wrote a series of articles on their work.

The climate of the age in terms of ideas in art and decoration was both reflected and created by these magazines. They were the purveyors of good taste. One of the early writers on the subject was Charles Eastlake, whose articles, *Hints on Household Taste*, had appeared in the *Cornhill Magazine* and were published in book form in England in 1867. Eastlake moves from room to room suggesting the best kind of decoration in each case. He has no sooner entered the front door, when he says 'there can be no doubt that the best mode of treating a hall-floor whether in town or country is to pave it with encaustic tiles. This branch of art manufacture is one of the most hopeful, in regard to taste, now carried on in the country.'[15] He commends tiles as the best form of decoration because they are cheap, durable and beautiful; not too much colour should be used and for floors two matching shades are best. He singles out Godwin's tiles as being noted for their artistic quality of colour and design. But for variety and skill Maw & Co. were, in his opinion, unrivalled. Remarks of this sort sent every refined person into a frenzy. Why were there no tiles in the hallway? Then, as now, the consumer was quickly persuaded to buy something new and fashionable. So there was only one thing for it. The lady of the house set off for the ironmonger and asked to see a tile catalogue from Godwin's or Maw's. A great deal of care and attention went into the production of these catalogues; with clear layouts and good colour printing they were undoubtedly the best medium for selling tiles.

The tile catalogues give a good idea of the designs that were available for the popular market. A Maw's catalogue illustrates:

Majolica and Enamelled Tiles, white and variously tinted Glazed Tiles, Decorated Glazed and Hand Painted Art Tiles, Glazed Encaustic, Incised, Enamelled, Pâte sur Pâte, Lustred and Gilt tiles, Architectural Enrichments etc. For hearths, fireplaces, wall linings, baths, friezes, skirtings, inscriptions, flower boxes, cabinet work etc.—Encaustic, Geometric, Mosaic etc. for Halls, Corridors, Passages, Conservatories, Churches, Cemetery Chapels, Porches, Gangways, Footpaths, Porticoes, Verandahs, Balconies, Ships' Galleys etc.

With the exception of the floor layouts these catalogues show individual designs, mostly for six-inch-square tiles, such as are commonly found in Victorian fireplaces and hearth surrounds (plate 19). Some of the designs are continuous over three or four tiles, set vertically or horizontally. Sunflowers growing in pots were a popular motif and the influence of Japanese taste is evident in some of the designs (plates 67 & 68). Several ranges of tiles were produced with wild flowers: hawthorn, bramble, violets, primroses, lilies. Such tiles could be applied not only to fireplaces; they served the same decorative function in the back of a wash-stand or as a part of a repeating pattern on the wall.

At their best they were an attractive form of ornament and answered the demand for tiles that were colourful and picturesque. However, it is one of the exigencies of industrial production that not everybody will work to the same high standard. Unquestionably a great number of tiles were made that were bad from any point of view. This did not go unnoticed and one critic, writing about the design of ceramic tiles, says:

Although latterly artists of high standing have exerted themselves admirably on its behalf they have to fight against an immense amount of misunderstanding caused by the lamentable want of taste shown by the lower class of manufacturers. A vast number of designs which have been put on the market cannot be accepted as in any sense worthy of even momentary consideration . . . they are feebly imagined, poorly executed and wanting in most of the essential attributes of true decoration . . . [they are] made in unnecessary profusion and sold freely to a large class of customers. They are to be met with constantly in private homes where they are used to ornament fireplaces and mantelpieces and to give a touch of spurious elegance to common-place rooms; and for the most part they are flagrantly unfitted by their crudity of colouring and weakness of design for any such application. These minor details of domestic decoration, when treated by a man of taste and not by a speculating builder, can, however, be made significant enough and a perception of this fact is slowly spreading. As it grows it will diminish the careless demand for the bad work and will allow the finer qualities of the art to gain the attention that is due to them.[16]

Many of the tiles produced were of poor quality; under the guise of being 'artistic' many were bought (and probably enjoyed) by a gullible public simply because they were fashionable.

The Art Movement played a vital role in the growth of the industry and the fashion for tiles. It is known that quite a number of new firms were established during the 1860s: Godwin's started in 1861, Malkin Edge and Co. was established in 1866 and in the next few years many others also went into production (see 'British tile manufacturers and marks', page 156). But they began by making encaustic and geometric tiles, in most cases, since there was an established market. Minton's had started transfer printing tiles in about 1850 but it was twenty years before any great number were made. The decorative wall tiles did not come into general use until the beginning of the 1870s, inspired by the Art Movement. Again the Royal family provide a guide as to what was happening. *The Illustrated London News* 27 July 1861 announced that 'the new Royal Dairy at Frogmore, near Windsor, just completed, is a perfect gem of taste and art'. Apart from the encaustic tiles on the floor, the ceramic decorations at Frogmore were mostly modelled in majolica ware—fountains and bas-reliefs representing the four seasons and various agricultural subjects. The walls were decorated with litho-printed tiles, with flat colour patterns that were similar to the encaustic tiles. The description ends by remarking that 'this chaste little work affords another proof of the delicate taste and refined judgement of the Queen and her consort'. That the words 'taste' and 'refined' should be associated with tiles is significant. In the 1870s, the popular market was controlled by the ideal of the Aesthetic Movement; refinement and good taste were of great importance.

During the last twenty-five years of the century more tiles were produced, and for a greater variety of purposes, than ever before. The pioneering work of the early years of Victoria's reign now paid a dividend that made the Stoke tilemasters wealthy men. In 1888 Maw's became a limited liability company and the family bought themselves out for £67,000. Most of the money was paid in the form of 60,000 £1 shares. The minute book for 13 November of that year recorded that 'the condition of the business was discussed and was considered to be very satisfactory, the manufacturing output had been much larger than was anticipated but not equal to the demands. It was resolved to make such further outlay of capital for kilns, buildings and other purposes as the board thought advisable.' At this time the two senior members of the family held most of the shares and for several years the only recorded business discussed at the directors' meeting was the agreement to pay a ten per cent dividend. Business was booming.

Maw's became the largest single tile manufacturer and they did so partially at the expense of Minton's. In 1868 Michael Hollins had gained sole ownership of the business making floor tiles and Colin Campbell continued to produce the famous Minton china. But the settlement proved difficult and there were court cases in 1871 and 1875 when the right to use the celebrated name of 'Minton' was in dispute (see Appendix). This publicity tarnished the image of the firms concerned and Hollins was already manufacturing in opposition to Robert Minton Taylor who for a few years had been a partner in the firm. In addition to this, although they made no floor tiles, Minton's China Works were also making glazed and decorated tiles—so there were three firms using the name of Minton on tiles. The situation was complicated and although the difficulty was resolved in Hollins's favour by the court decision of 1875, the company was clearly losing business as a result of the confusion. Messrs Campbell and Taylor later established the Campbell Brick and Tile Co. and there can be no doubt that this new company quickly became successful both in making and marketing tiles. Maw's and all the other manufacturers drew benefit from this family quarrel. But since the market for commercially produced tiles was increasing at such a prodigious rate the loss in trade was only relative. There was plenty of work for everyone. A report on the *Great Industries of Great Britain*, published in December 1879, indicates the scale of production at this time. With their long-standing reputation, Minton, Hollins & Co. were chosen to represent the tile makers in the ceramics section and the writer describes the pottery with the enthusiasm of a man dedicated to the glorification of British industry:

In Shelton New Road, Stoke-on-Trent, and not far from the centre of that town, stand the celebrated tile works of Messrs Minton, Hollins & Co. The street lies near the foot of a range of hills that run in an undulating line along the eastern side of the Potteries. The works occupy the greater portion of one side of this thoroughfare, and externally resemble something between a substantially built school and a plain unpretending chapel. But turning through a gateway towards the end of a long block of clean redbrick buildings the idea that you are entering either the portals of knowledge or the precincts of religious devotion cannot for an instant be entertained. These are but the offices of the firm, which shut out from the ordinary gaze the several square blocks of shopping which lie beyond them. Each range is in itself a small works, but when viewed in conjunction with the others, when the throbbing of machinery is heard, and the hum of strongly-marshalled labour arises, and the great kilns on every side belch forth their inky billows of smoke, it is clear that this is not exactly the quiet haunt of man. It is even clearer still when, turning sharply to the left and ascending the stairs that lead to corridor on corridor of offices, you see the walls covered with tiles of many designs, but all bearing as the central ornament the monogram of the firm. In every passage, at every turning, in every angle, and in every corner, they are still before you, and the floor on which you tread is inlaid with some of those famous encaustic tiles which, while recalling the classical tesselated pavement, remind one of the world-wide renown which their manufacture has achieved for Messrs Minton, Hollins & Co. The walls inside some of the offices are relieved with tiles and on the tables and mantel-pieces in odd corners you are confronted with these square slabs of clay; some, with their choice ornamentation, evoking admiration, others appealing to your ideas of neatness, and all reminding the beholder of the power and resources of the potter's art. The business, which was established in 1840 by the late Mr Herbert Minton, and his nephew, Mr M. D. Hollins, who is now the absolute proprietor of the place, was at that period very different to what it is now. Then the tilemaking was carried on in Church Street, but owing to the development of trade and the popularity which tiles attained this place was found totally inadequate for manufacturing purposes. Then the existing building, covering an area of more than seven acres, and giving employment to eight hundred hands, was erected, with every facility, as will be shown, for conducting an extensive trade, and with sufficient resources, both manual and mechanical, to meet the most pressing demands of busy periods. For a long time and until about ten years since, the interests of the firm under notice were identical with those of Messrs Minton, the no less celebrated manufacturer of porcelain. On passing through the large open space, on both sides of which are shops several stories high, it will be noticed that there are fourteen firing ovens of exceptional dimensions, and there are six more at another works close by. Here, too, we catch a glimpse of the vast and ponderous machinery which gives motive force to this industrial hive, and entering the mills, we at once observe the large quantities of earthy material ready for pulverization, or, with certain chemical ingredients, ready to be reduced into soft, moist clay.[17]

Going through the various 'shops' the writer describes the manufacturing process (see chapter 4). There were sixty presses in constant use, each producing over one thousand articles in a day, that is, about one and a half million items each month. When these figures are multiplied by the number of firms manufacturing tiles it is difficult to conceive exactly how all the tiles were used. A proportion were always lost in firing, of course, and the figures do apply to all types of ceramic tiles, including mosaics. Furnival records that another manufacturer, Edwards of Ruabon, started production as a complete novice, with the assistance of a man and two boys: by the turn of the century a thousand people were employed and the firm was producing two million articles per month. Many of these tiles were probably plain white and undecorated and so do not qualify for present consideration: T. & R. Boote's, for instance, tiled the Blackwall Tunnel (built 1892–7) which is over 2000 ft long and 24 ft in diameter and used somewhere in the region of half a million plain white tiles. However, this contract probably only represented a couple of months work for the firm.

Decorated tiles formed the most interesting part of the production in the nineteenth century. The same report concludes the description of the Minton, Hollins factory with a visit to the painting shop:

With the evidence of the fact so constantly before us, it is almost unnecessary to say that the decoration and ornamentation of tiles have in these days reached such perfection as to come within the region of high art. While there is much meritous decoration produced by the printing process, it is in painting on china tiles, used for various purposes of ornamentation, and on fancy hearth-tiles, that the most artistic effect is realized. The delicate and chaste painting on slabs of china is almost invariably performed by ladies with a skill that compares favourably with similar, and much more pretentious work on canvas. The painting of costly tiles—tiles which form bright pictures of the hearth that do not readily face—is always effected in their biscuit state. These tiles are passed into the department of the artists, and these gentlemen place them upon their easels, and with the colours which have been so carefully prepared transform the plain squares of clay into lovely pictures. The firing necessary to indelibly fix the colours lasts many hours. The tiles, after firing, are returned to the artists, who in putting the several pieces together can observe the general effect of their work, and very pleasing it is. For instance at one end of the long room, sacred to the artist's fancy, may be found a series of tiles illustrative of horses' and dogs' heads. They are drawn with such breadth, vigour, faithfulness, and animation, as to recall the skill of Rosa Bonheur [an animal painter who enjoyed a considerable reputation (born 1822)].

Further on may be seen tiles representing birds of many-hued plumage, which testify to the marked care with which the painter has portrayed these bright-winged creatures. At the other end of the room there are tiles treated in a conventional manner; whilst in the middle of the place there may be noticed a large number of pieces, perhaps more than forty, of tile-work, which when they are 'fitted up in the destined fireplace will indeed beautify that hearth. The central design is a group of rose leaves—every blushing petal being minutely figured—with a border of dead leaves, the flowers being painted as only true artists can render them. When finished, the tiles are taken to the large warehouses, and there they are stacked in their tens of thousands.

A great many artists were involved in the decoration of the tiles. Even those that were transfer printed were often 'filled in' by hand. This was rather a mechanical process and involved little more than colouring sections, like filling in a child's drawing book. But most of the potteries were also producing finely decorated tiles that were painted by hand, either as a group to make up an illustrative panel, such as the one described, or individually like the Copeland tiles illustrated (plate 29). Basically the situation was ruled by economics: any firm manufactured a full range of tiles that were bought by a variety of customers. Copeland's specialized in making a few hand-made tiles decorated by skilful painters. R. J. Abraham (1850–1925) was one of their chief designers (plate 63) and his work has a charm that matches anything produced by his contemporaries. Other firms, like Minton, Hollins's and Maw's, manufactured a wide range of mass-produced tiles for the popular market and also specialized in decorative panels for architectural use, such as those painted by Albert Slater (plate 103). Many of the tile manufacturers, Minton's in particular, took great pains to employ gifted designers to paint fine tiles and to undertake research into the skills of tile making. Leon Arnoux has already been mentioned for his perseverance in rediscovering the secrets of the old Arabic glazes in the fifties. But until about 1870 the tile designers were mostly architects who, like Pugin, wanted to use tiles in their buildings and thought themselves best equipped to design them. The paintresses, though usually skilful and gifted, were limited in their abilities, if only because they were limited in experience, and the majority were employed on routine work. At Minton's China Works the chief designers were Frenchmen. The American *Artist and Journal of Home Culture* was amused by the Englishness of Minton's tiles when so many of the artists were French. In fact only seven of the 140 artists employed were foreigners but they happened to hold important positions: Marc Louis Solon, who joined in 1870, was one of the chief painters; M. Reuter (Swiss) was first assistant designer to M. Arnoux, and M. Leroux was one of the artist decorators. Solon's work, though his themes were often sentimental, was extremely accomplished and his *pâte sur pâte* (see page 78) panels command respect for their skill and ingenuity.

There can be no doubt that many of the designs, such as the sunflower and the lily, symbols of the Aesthetic Movement, were borrowed from other fields of art. Japanese scenes and motifs were often copied from imported goods such as those sold by Liberty & Co. (established 1875). Painted tiles in imitation of Burne-Jones, were made by Simpson's, and Maw's produced a range of 'Persian Ware', similar to William De Morgan's work. William Morris, who like De Morgan had very little love for the industrial potters, also made an unwitting contribution to their pattern books and there are several designs evocative of Morris's chintz wallpapers. But such tiles were made in response to a popular demand. It is surprising that so few designers of Morris's or De Morgan's calibre were involved in the problems of mass-production at this time. Their work was popular and was instrumental in forming public taste; yet the production of their own efforts could never satisfy the demand that they helped to create. They refused to have anything to do with the industrial potters, and so the market was open to imitations. Some of these were good and some of them were bad; it depended on the individual manufacturer. But Minton, Hollins's, Maw's or Simpson's were at least as expert, technically, as De Morgan and it is difficult to understand why he refused to sell his designs to these firms and take advantage of their commercial production techniques. If the best designers, at any time, do not work for the largest number of people then a cheap and inferior imitation of their work will appear on the popular market. But quality and quantity are not incompatible, as the work of the best of the nineteenth-century tile makers demonstrates.

Towards the end of the century a few men were beginning to grapple with this problem. Lewis F. Day, for instance, who was a distinguished designer in many fields, undertook designs for Maw's, Pilkington's and J. C. Edwards. In many ways he was one of the most clear-headed thinkers of his time and wrote a good many articles about design. He almost always made some reference to tiles. Writing for the *Art Journal* in 1895, he laments that 'the sample sheets from the large producers, far from showing any originality, invention or enterprise, look on the whole very much alike. It is as if the makers acted largely on the belief that only what has sold is likely to sell, serenely assuming that there was no reason why, because one of them had a happy thought, the rest of them should not hasten to benefit by it if they could.'[18]

Day goes on to suggest ways of distinguishing the quality of workmanship. There is a great deal of difference between colours flowing together in the glaze and colours mixing together messily after being 'sploshed on'. It is a matter of accuracy. There is no need for 'hard-edge' work. It is obvious when the painter has not taken reasonable care over an individual tile. As for the designs themselves, Lewis Day laments the poor quality and lack of artistry in so many of them. He devoted a great deal of effort to the abstraction of decorative motif from natural forms and the qualities of form and line; his work is an interesting prelude to Art Nouveau. But only few other designers followed his involvement in the subject (plate 28). He singles out Minton, Hollins's here on the ground that although they had perfected the technical aspects of production most of their tiles were lagging behind in terms of art and design. They were trading on their reputation and were out of touch with current ideas.

In 1893, Owen Carter wrote *On Designing Tiles*, largely intended as a handbook for students. He observed that there was a heavy demand for printed tiles at that time and that many of the smaller firms either copied patterns or employed outside designers and would pay between 7s 6d and 15s for a design. The designs would have been purchased outright and no records are available to enable identification of the young artists who did them. But it is known that a number of professional designers did freelance work for some manufacturers. Walter Crane undertook work for several firms, notably Pilkington's (plate 51). In 1880 Crane became Art Superintendent of the London Decorating Co. which specialized in encaustic tiles; his skill as a designer was matched by his involvement in commerce and he was never afraid to capitalize on the popularity of his designs. C. F. A. Voysey worked in the same way and one of his designs called 'ornamental tree' was drawn on tiles by Pilkington's but was also marked down for Essex & Co., the wallpaper manufacturers. Burne-Jones, who was probably more successful in the applied arts (designing stained-glass windows) than he was as a painter, had his designs painted on ceramic plaques by the Della Robbia Pottery Co. (established 1894). It is important to note, however, that in this case the tiles were made entirely by hand.

Another designer was J. Moyr Smith. He was retained by Minton's (China Works) during the seventies and eighties and produced a large number of tiles that were all transfer printed and produced in a range of colours. Twelve subjects illustrated Thomson's *Seasons* (Autumn: 'crowned with sickle and the wheaten sheaf'; Reaping: 'Each by the lass that he loves, To bear the rougher part, and mitigate, By nameless gentle offices, her toil', and so on). Another series of twelve tiles by Moyr Smith were illustrations from *Waverley*. These and other designs like the Shakespeare tiles, fable subjects and illustrations to Tennyson's *Idylls of the King* distinguished Minton's range of tiles from those of any other manufacturer (plate 86). Another of Minton's designers, who received considerable contemporary recognition, was Leon V. Solon, the son of M. L. Solon whose work at Minton's was mentioned above. Solon left art school in about 1896 and *The Studio* followed his work with much interest and enthusiasm, remarking that for him 'the possibility of new effects appears to be endless'. Although many other companies continued to produce decorative wall tiles, mainly with plain coloured glazes (majolica), men like Solon had completely changed the definition of 'tile' by the turn of the century.* Solon's work was largely figurative and tile production of this sort was no longer a matter of design but ceramic painting of a new and highly technical kind (plates 56 and 57). But these tiles were, perhaps, a little too sophisticated for the English market and Minton's tile trade dwindled after 1900.

* Solon later emigrated to America and worked for the American Encaustic Tiling Co. of Zanesville, Ohio.

44

4 Methods of production

The Craft Revival, which was so important in terms of nineteenth-century art and design, has overshadowed many of the remarkable inventions of the late Industrial Revolution. While William Morris looked back to the traditions of medieval craftsmanship, many other men managed to work, successfully, within the confines of their own times. There was no real difference between rediscovery and invention: they both employed the same ingenuity. But while the Victorian artist-craftsmen were bent on reviving old ideas and techniques, the industrial manufacturers were concerned with inventing new and more profitable methods of producing their goods. In the case of tiles the two outlooks were complementary. When Herbert Minton started making encaustic tiles in 1830, he was working as a craftsman, reviving an ancient and forgotten skill. He was constantly aware, however, of the possibilities of industrial production. But rather than seeing commercial considerations as a conflicting interest, he welcomed them as the natural outcome of his labours. It is almost as though he changed Morris's dictum ('Think of your material. Don't paint anything on pottery save what can be painted only on pottery.'[19]) and made it 'Think of your machine. Don't make anything by machine save only what can best be made by machine.' The essential uniformity of the dimensions of ceramic tiles is perfectly suited to machine production. Since any irregularity becomes more pronounced in a repeated pattern, it is almost essential to make tiles mechanically. Only then can the dimensions begin to be guaranteed.*

The Cistercian monks, who were the medieval tile makers, worked by hand. They flattened the clay and cut the pieces to shape. But even they availed themselves of such mechanical aids as they could devise and the pattern was indented in the clay with a wooden mould, carved in relief. This ensured the accuracy of the pattern. The man best equipped to draw and carve would have made the mould and his less gifted companions would have used it as a former for their work. The slab had to be dried and then the intaglio pattern was filled with pipe-clay. After a further drying period the tile was shaved flat. A glaze of sand and lead ore was sprinkled on and then the tiles were fired. This 'honey-glaze', as it is sometimes called, gave a yellowish tinge to the white pipe-clay and protected the tile from dirt and erosion. It seems likely that each monastery made its own tiles, using local clays wherever possible.

Neither Minton nor Wright could have known much more about the medieval encaustic tiles. It was not difficult to form the basic tile shape. The complications arose when the technical problems of clay types and

* In fact, even dust-pressed tiles had to be graded for size, since the dimensions varied according to the temperature in any part of the kiln, and variations in the clay.

firing techniques had to be solved. The monastic potters probably drew on a long tradition of specialized local knowledge. But for Minton, Wright's patent of 1830 established little more than the right to the idea of making encaustic tiles; there was nothing to guide him except the results of continuous and innumerable experiments. This empirical approach took a long time. It was five years before he had even a few tiles that were satisfactory. If nothing went wrong during the drying stages, then the tiles could be tested in the kiln. But a kiln took just over a week to fire completely. There were so many variables in the experiments that it was a matter of luck how quickly he stumbled on the right results. A large proportion of the tiles were likely to be destroyed during the firing and Jewitt records (see page 14) that Minton felt delighted if only a small number of the 700 that made up a kiln-load were unspoiled. The experience needed to perfect the process could only be bought with patience and persistence. Minton had these qualities and his eventual success was a triumph that he well deserved.

The manufacture of a tile begins when the clay is 'won' from the pits, some of which were opencast, others were some two hundred feet or more below the ground. The basic red clays that are natural to Stoke were combined with other clays and additives to make the correct mixture for the body of the tile. Two clays of the same chemical composition might behave totally differently in the kiln and the most satisfactory combination for all purposes could only be ascertained by large-scale experiments.*

The mixture for the tile body might contain coloured marls, or ball clay, kaolin (china clay), flint, and other substances. Additional clays were needed to make the various appliances used in different parts of the operation (such as the 'bats', 'cranks' and 'saggars'). Several chemicals were also used for colouring purposes. The difficulty was to find the right combination of these elements to ensure that the tiles eventually had the properties required. With encaustic tiles the chief problem, once accurate colours were obtained, was to ensure that the different clays on the surface of the tile fused together during the firing. It was a common failure for the inlaid section to shrink away from the body, owing to the differential contraction of the two materials. Warping and cracking would often occur during the drying stage and yet the mixture that gave rise to this failure may well have behaved perfectly satisfactorily in the kiln.

Wright had not resolved many of the technical problems when Minton bought the patent in 1830. Few details are available to give clues as to exactly how he managed to perfect the technique but by 1844, when the patent was elaborated and renewed, the manufacturing process for encaustic tiles was as follows. The clay mixture was first cleaned and

---

* When Maw & Co. bought the tile business in Worcester, they tried for a couple of years to work there, but the local clays proved to be unsuitable. On moving to Broseley in the Ironbridge Gorge, Maw undertook a comprehensive survey of clays and allied materials to be found in Britain; he studied some 700 specimens and 120 different kinds of clay. It was a valuable report and he presented it to the Museum of Practical Geology in London.

purified. Unwanted mineral traces had to be removed since they might stain the tile or set up a chemical reaction during the firing. The flints and larger grade materials were ground and in the correct proportions the different parts of the mixture were run together and water added to make what was called 'slip'. The slip was sieved, so that only the fine suspended particles were used. The mixture was then dried on plaster bats which absorbed the water to bring it to a plastic state. After going through a pug-mill the clay was flattened and forced into a metal frame that shaped each tile. The frame had to be oversize to allow for shrinkage when the clay dried—a $6\frac{5}{8}$ in. square of wet clay reduced to approximately 6 in. square when the tile was finished. The relief pattern that formed the intaglio in the clay was placed at the bottom of the frame. A layer of fine clay was laid first, about $\frac{1}{4}$ in. deep, which would eventually form the face of the tile. A band of coarser clay was then pressed into the frame and covered with another $\frac{1}{4}$ in. layer of fine clay. This sandwiching had a dual purpose: most important, it helped to prevent warping and secondly it meant that, although the surface of the tile was fine and the image perfect, the band of coarser clay ensured that the body of the tile was robust. To complete the formation of the slab, a plate was put over the top of the frame and the layers of clay compacted together.

The frame was then inverted and the plaster of paris die was removed. The top surface of the tile was then exposed with the pattern indented into the clay. After a period of drying, coloured slip (a solution of fine white clay, which could be coloured with chemical ingredients) was poured on to the tile and the intaglio pattern filled. The channels were overfilled to allow for shrinkage and at this stage the tile would have appeared very messy. After three days of drying, the surface of the tile was scraped clean and flat and the design could be seen, with sharp, clear edges. The tile was then removed from its frame and put on a shelf in the drying house for between two and three weeks before firing.

The process, as it has been described here, was essentially manual. A few machines helped with the preparing of the clay but that was the case with the manufacture of all earthenware at this time. Gradually, however, the facilities of nineteenth-century engineering were applied to the process and the patents that were taken out show the major stages in this development, although there was a constant progress of ideas and minor changes. In the 1830s each tile was cleaned and levelled by hand. Presumably a long, sharp blade was scraped across the surface, using the sides of the iron frame to keep the level constant. By the time the patent was renewed in 1844, this process was done by machine. The tiles were passed beneath a rotating cutter that shaved the surface down, almost instantaneously, to a constant depth, leaving a perfectly smooth face. When this was done by hand it was easy for the surface of the tile to be slightly damaged; the machine gave a uniform and perfect finish every time. To the exponents of the Craft Tradition this was not a desirable feature. Perhaps part of the charm of the original encaustic tiles was their irregularity and minor flaws. Certainly in the seventies *The Builder* makes the criticism that encaustic tiles are far too spick and span and that they look like copy-book patterns. The work of Maw & Co. (in association with Simpson's) in the Lady Chapel of St Mary Redcliffe's, Bristol, was cited as an attractive example of a rougher finish.* These tiles, richly coloured in yellow, green and black were made in strict imitation of the old medieval examples and an attempt was made to prevent the pattern being too true. This was a reversal of the original requirements. Minton aimed to make the tiles perfectly regular and precise. It is a measure of his success that the criticism was made.

Until 1855, a good working day for one man produced between 200 and 220 moulded six-inch encaustic tiles in two colours. Single coloured quarry and wall tiles could be made from plastic clay at a rate of up to about 800 a day. In 1855, Samuel Barlow Wright and Henry Thomas Greene invented a mechanical process for forming wet clay encaustic tiles. With the pattern indented but not filled, plastic clay slabs could be cut at a rate of about twenty a minute, so that several thousand slabs might be cut during a full working day, although it is highly improbable that anything like that number were actually made at this date. Three pug-mills were set in a row; the central mill produced coarse clay and was flanked by two mills extruding fine clay. They discharged between two rollers and the strips of clay were flattened and pressed together to form a continuous slab, with the correct depth of coarse clay sandwiched between the fine. A belt, travelling at a speed of twelve feet per minute carried the flat strip under a cylindrical roller which had a die set into it. The roller turned as the clay passed beneath it and as it did so the intaglio was impressed into the clay. A guillotine then cut the slabs to the required size. The slip was applied in the same way as before. After a further dimension trim and drying, the tile was ready to be fired.

In 1863 Boulton and Worthington patented a method for making encaustic tiles from clay dust rather than plastic clay. But before considering this new invention, it is as well to look at Prosser's patent of 1840 on which it was based. The background to Prosser's patent has already been described (see page 16); the press that he designed for making ceramic buttons was quickly converted to make ceramic tiles and tesserae. The clay mix was not quite the same for wall tiles, since different properties were required. A white body was important, particularly for underglaze decoration and this was achieved partly by including a larger proportion of calcined flint. The clay was cleaned and washed in the same way, but was dried for much longer than was necessary for the plastic clay process. This was done in heated troughs of refractory material. It was important to get exactly the right water content, but the clay felt dry and so it was often called 'dust'. This clay dust required additional grinding after it left the drying beds, to ensure that it was perfectly smooth and free from lumps. It had a

---

* A few years ago, in a fit of modernization, a carpet was laid in the Lady Chapel and, although they are still there, the tiles cannot be seen.

29 Copeland, transfer-printed outline hand-coloured; 1878. Although the tiles are attractive, the designs are not particularly suited to the medium. The medieval minstrels, watched over by sunflowers are typical of the period. Collection H. & R. Johnson-Richards.

30 Bottle ovens at the Gladstone Pottery, Longton, Staffordshire. This old 'pot-bank', built *c*. 1850, has been restored by the Staffordshire Pottery Industry Preservation Trust as a 'living museum'. The kilns, once so characteristic of the city's skyline, are among the few that remain in Stoke-on-Trent. H. & R. Johnson-Richards.

31 Low's Art Tile Works, Chelsea, Massachusetts. Although the kilns were made of fire-bricks, most of the buildings were constructed in wood — it is not surprising that so many of the early American potteries were gutted by fire. By permission Victoria & Albert Museum, London.

32 An old photograph of Longton, one of the Six Towns of North Staffordshire. Blakes, Hanley, Stoke-on-Trent.

33 In the nineteenth century the local marls were often dug from pits close to the pottery. Blakes, Hanley, Stoke-on-Trent.

34 Lead mould used to emboss the surface of dust pressed tiles (plate 27). By permission City Museum, Stoke-on-Trent.

35 Dust press in operation; by turning the wheel, a die was lowered on to the mould to compress the clay dust. By permission Victoria & Albert Museum, London.

36 Majolica tiles: *top left*: no marks, brown with central square green; *c.* 1895. *top right*: no marks, dark chocolate with yellow centre; *c.* 1890. *middle left*: no marks, green. *middle right*: Pilkington's, 1894; the pattern has the appearance of tube-lining but was dust pressed. Design in blue and green, possibly by J. Chambers. *bottom left*: Maw & Co., *c.* 1880; yellow glaze, unimaginative colouring of an attractive design. *bottom right*: Sherwin & Cotton, *c.* 1895; green.

37 Majolica tiles: *top left*: no marks, brown, green and blue. *top right*: no marks, olive with red roundels. *middle left*: no marks, brown with centre in high relief, 1891. *middle right*: 'C*B', *c.* 1895; olive, green, plum and yellow. *bottom left*: no marks, dark green art nouveau motif; *c.* 1905. *bottom right*: T. & R. Boote, *c.* 1880; green.

38 Doulton & Co., *c.* 1875; sgraffito panel of six tiles by Hannah Barlow who enjoyed a considerable reputation for such vivid animal designs. Here two coats of slip were applied over the drab body; when the design was etched into clay the blue undercoat gave greater strength to the line. Sotheby & Co., London.

39 Minton's China Works, c. 1885; 'The Punishment of the Cupids' - a *pâte sur pâte* plaque by M. L. Solon, 7 x 10 in. The design was painted on to the olive-green body in very thin coats of white slip. Sotheby & Co., London.

40 Rookwood Pottery Co., 1907; Spring and Winter, two from a set of four panels illustrating the seasons. Each panel is composed of thirty tiles, 91 x 29 in. Cincinnati Art Museum, Ohio.

41

42

41 American Encaustic Tiling Co., *c.* 1895; terracotta panel by Herman Mueller, 16 x 16 in. Cincinnati Art Museum, Ohio.

42 American Encaustic Tiling Co., *c.* 1905. Cincinnati Art Museum, Ohio.

43 The mark on the back of the plaque, 'Frogs Dancing'. Cincinnati Art Museum, Ohio.

44 American Encaustic Tiling Co., polychrome tile with white ground, 4 in. Smithsonian Institution, Washington DC.

43

44

45 Transfer-printed tiles. *top left:* 'R11', brown transfer hand-coloured blue and green. *top middle:* no marks, blue. *top right:* embossed mark 'No 2', blue. *middle left:* Minton's China Works, No 2697, brown transfer hand-coloured pink and yellow. *middle:* 'S636', grey body with brown and black transfer hand-coloured yellow, green and white. *middle right:* 'COV 585' brown transfer hand-coloured brown, grey and yellow. *bottom left:* embossed 'England' and '3', brown. *bottom middle:* no marks, brown transfer hand-coloured blue, brown and green. *bottom right:* 'A32', brown transfer hand-coloured pink and greens, 1888.

46 Cambridge Art Tile Works. Majolica tiles such as these were particularly popular in America. Smithsonian Institution, Washington DC.

47 *top left*: no marks, hand-coloured yellow and pink on green transfer. *top right*: Wedgwood, pink transfer. *middle left*: no marks, brown transfer hand-coloured yellow and browns. *middle right*: no marks, brown transfer hand-coloured yellow, red and green, *c.* 1895. *bottom left*: no marks, brown transfer hand-coloured yellows and blues. *bottom right*: Burmantoft's, 'G887', brown transfer hand-coloured pink and green with pale blue border, *c.* 1885.

48 The lavatories adjacent to the old Refreshment Rooms at the Victoria & Albert Museum, London. The tiles were made by Minton, Hollins & Co., *c*. 1868, using an airbrush and stencil. By permission Victoria & Albert Museum, London.

49 Detail of plate 48. The airbrush produces a speckled finish and the stencil leaves a rather ragged edge to the design. By permission Victoria & Albert Museum, London.

50 *top row left to right*: Craven Dunnill, *c.* 1890; hand-painted through stencil. Minton, Hollins & Co., *c.* 1885; black transfer pattern from *Aesop's Fables* with inglaze colouring. J. C. Edwards, *c.* 1890; lustre tile. Malkin, Edge & Co., *c.* 1885; transfer print. *second row*: Chamberlain's of Worcester, *c.* 1845; encaustic tile. Maw & Co., *c.* 1870; litho-printed transfer. Copeland, 1878; transfer-printed outline hand-coloured. No marks, transfer print. *third row*: William De Morgan, *c.* 1875; hand-painted design. Minton, Hollins & Co., *c.* 1880; 'Wednesday's child is full of woe'. Maw & Co., *c.* 1880; transfer print. No marks, litho-printed transfer. *bottom row*: Malkin, Edge & Co., *c.* 1890; transfer print. W. B. Simpson & Sons, 1881; transfer print with hand-colouring under- and overglaze. Minton's China Works, 1898; transfer print. Wedgwood, transfer print. Collection H. & R. Johnson-Richards.

51 *top left and right*: Pilkington's, 1902; two of a series of six tube-lined tiles designed by Walter Crane. Victoria and Albert Museum, London. *bottom right*: no marks, polychrome design using tube-lined technique.

52 Sherwin & Cotton, *c.* 1890; 8½ x 6 in. One of a series depicting contemporary leaders and politicians. 'Matene. Te. Nga' was a Maori chief and the tile is thought to commemorate a visit he paid to Queen Victoria. The relief was moulded by a photographic process. Sotheby & Co., London.

53 Sherwin & Cotton, *c.* 1890; 12 x 6 in. One of a series with stags in Highland glens, glazed green or brown. Sotheby & Co., London.

54 Lustre tiles: *top left*: no marks, *c.* 1890. Collection H. & R. Johnson-Richards. *top right*: J. C. Edwards, *c.* 1890; designed by Lewis F. Day. By permission Victoria & Albert Museum, London. *bottom left*: William De Morgan, *c.* 1873 (Chelsea period); painted on biscuit imported from Holland. Collection H. & R. Johnson-Richards. *bottom right*: William De Morgan, *c.* 1875; 8 in. Collection H. & R. Johnson-Richards.

55 Details from various tiles showing faults that can occur. *top left:* a crack in an encaustic tile. *top right:* pinholes caused by impurities in the body of the tile which blow through the glaze and leave a hole unhealed. *middle left:* a nipped corner — here the tile was faulty before firing but, rather than waste the biscuit, it was decorated and sold as a 'second'. *middle right:* run glaze, caused by the tile being set unevenly in the kiln; this is a very poor quality tile. *bottom left:* kiln dirty — a particle of clay, probably from a saggar, has dropped on to the face of the tile. *bottom right:* crazing — a fault frequently found in majolica tiles because of the thickness of the glaze. It is usually caused by dampness which makes the biscuit expand and so breaks the glaze.

 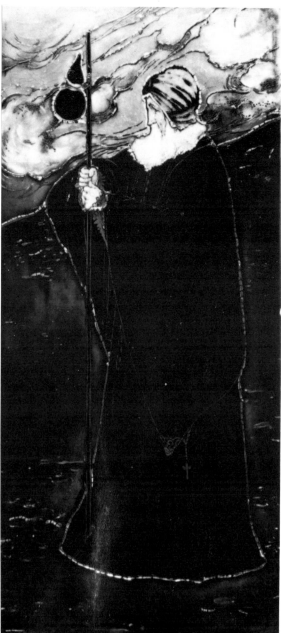

56 Minton's China Works, 1902; hand-painted polychrome design on plaque made from plastic clay, 19¼ x 11 in. Probably a trial piece, by Leon V. Solon. Sotheby & Co., London.

57 Minton's China Works, *c*. 1900; 'The Pilgrim' by L. V. Solon, 14 x 16 in. Solon used novel and elaborate techniques in his tile paintings and had a reputation for this type of experimental work at the turn of the century. Sotheby & Co., London.

58 *top left:* no marks, majolica tile with pink and green glazes. *top right:* no marks, polychrome majolica tile with brown background. *middle left:* Wedgwood Patent Impressed Tile, 1884; relief pattern on white ground in olive and blues. Collection Ian Craig. *middle right:* Wedgwood Patent Impressed Tile, 1884; grey body with relief pattern in brown, green and white. *bottom left:* Maw & Co., *c.* 1875; brown and olive probably sprayed through a stencil. Collection Ian Craig. *bottom right:* Doulton & Co., *c.* 1880; two-tone blue litho-printed transfer. By permission Susan Ford.

59 Transfer-printed tiles. *top left:* 'COV No 339', brown. *top middle:* embossed 'R', 'England' and '29', red. *top right:* no marks, brown transfer hand-coloured pink, yellow and blue. *middle left:* Copeland, buff body, brown transfer, 1884. *middle:* no marks, brown transfer hand-coloured blues, yellow and brown. *middle right:* '649' brown, 1896. *bottom left:* Copeland, blue litho-printed transfer. *bottom middle:* Wedgwood 'T528', brown transfer (this design was also printed in blue). *bottom right:* Wedgwood, stamped by Maple & Co., London (suppliers), black.

60 William De Morgan tiles: *left:* 1898, green and yellow. By permission City Museum, Stoke-on-Trent. *right: c.* 1895; purple, blues, white, yellow and greens, 8 in. Collection H. & R. Johnson-Richards.

61 William De Morgan tiles of the Sands End, Fulham period. Sotheby & Co., London. *left:* floral design predominantly blue and green, *c.* 1895. *middle:* green galleon from early Fulham period, 1888-97. *right:* green dodo, impressed DM98, 1898.

Opposite
62 De Morgan tiles, predominantly purple and green; probably from the Chelsea period 1872-82. One drawback of working entirely by hand was the irregularities both in the tile and the pattern. Here the biscuit is badly warped and the design does not match-up across the tiles. By permission Victoria & Albert Museum, London.

63 W. P. Jervis, hand-painted polychrome designs by R. J. Abraham; 6 in. Sotheby & Co., London.

62

63

64 Morris & Co., *c.* 1870; probably designed by Burne-Jones. By permission Victoria & Albert Museum, London.

natural cohesion and, when under pressure in the mould, it compacted to form a tile that could be handled without any further drying. The design of the press was modified on several occasions but it consisted basically of a metal plate that was lowered on to the bed by means of a screw thread. The clay dust was compressed between the surfaces as the plate was lowered. For a plain, flat-faced, wall tile, the plate was smooth, although the back of the tile was usually shaped or patterned to assist fixing. This 'key back' might also carry the manufacturer's name and trade-mark (for information on marks and patterned backs see 'British tile manufacturers and their marks', page 156). If the tile had a surface pattern, then a die was placed at the bottom of the mould. This plate or die was set to the correct level, according to the thickness required: for a $6 \times 6 \times \frac{3}{8}$ in. wall tile, just over $\frac{5}{8}$ in. of dust was put into the mould.

The presser wiped the plates clean with a greasy rag, filled the mould with dust clay and scraped the surface level. Then he slowly lowered the press by turning the large horizontal wheel at the top which was about six feet in diameter. This allowed the air to escape from the clay in the mould. The screw was then lifted slightly and quickly lowered again with a force of about thirty tons vertical pressure to compact and face the tile (plate 35). It was forced out of the mould by means of a foot-pedal and the operation was quickly repeated and another tile formed. Before being taken to the drying room, the tiles were removed for 'fettling': young girls brushed any surface dust from the tile and lightly sanded the edges with a dry washleather. The tiles were stacked six or eight high with 'setter' tiles, that had already been fired, between them. Two operatives, working one press, could produce over 1000 six-inch-square tiles a day in this way. Smaller presses, often operated by the women, were used for forming geometric tiles and tesserae for mosaics. Sixty of these presses were in operation at Minton, Hollins's, in 1879, although it is not known how many of these were for making six-inch tiles.

As the major manufacturer of machinery for tile-making in England, William Boulton, engineers at Burslem, near Stoke-on-Trent, in conjunction with Worthington and Messrs T. & R. Boote, developed a way of making encaustic tiles from clay dust, which was patented in 1863. It was possible, one might imagine, to make encaustic tiles under Prosser's patent, prior to this date, simply by putting a former at the bottom of the mould and increasing the depth of clay dust. But this was not done since the wet slip used to fill the indentations in the moulded tile would have seeped into the dry clay and spoiled it. The greatest single difficulty, however, would have been the imbalance in the water content of the two clays. The body of the tile would have been relatively dry and as the moisture evaporated from the inlaid section it would have pulled away from the body. The feature of the new process was that only dust clay was used. The patterned part of the tile was formed by using one or more copper plates which were perforated to the required design. Two guide pegs located the plate on the bed of the press and the hollows in this mould were filled with coloured clay dust. A die, whose relief pattern corresponded exactly to that of the plate, was then used to compress the clay, the ram coming down in such a way that the plate was removed as it returned. This left a pattern of compacted clay on the bed of the press. The box frame, such as was used for ordinary dust-pressed tiles, was now brought into position and filled with more clay, of a different colour, that would form the body. As this was compacted, in turn, the inlaid section was bedded perfectly into the face of the tile. The process was both quick and easy. More elaborate designs were possible—a second or third plate could fill different sections in a particular colour. Obviously, additional plates were also necessary if the lines of the design intersected at any point. The copper plates were about $\frac{1}{4}$ in. thick and very expensive to make. It was preferable, therefore, to use only the simplest patterns.

The great virtue of the Boulton and Worthington process was the speed with which the tiles could be made. It is probable, however, that the quality suffered as a result. It became more important that the design should suit the machine than the other way about. Perhaps this was a good thing—at least people didn't try to put delicate sunflower patterns on the floor. It also meant that encaustic tiles were available to a much wider market, since expense had always inhibited their more general use. The 1863 patent could best be applied to the production of two-colour tiles with a simple pattern and it is interesting that this is exactly what Charles Eastlake recommended, four years later, in his book *Hints on Household Taste*. But the dust process never ousted the wet clay method as far as encaustic tiles were concerned and the two ran side by side, each being used where most appropriate.

The majority, though not all, of the tile makers worked in the Six Towns of the North Staffordshire Potteries. They came from families who had lived and worked there for many generations. The clay beds and the proximity of coal for firing purposes made this district the traditional centre for the industry. That most of the potters did come from Stoke is important, for one particular reason. They all knew each other, friends, rivals or arch-enemies, nobody could do anything without all the others knowing about it. The patents became rather irrelevant in this context; instead of giving a man sole right to the use of the process, to the exclusion of his rivals, it is quite apparent that if anybody had a new idea, whether for manufacturing or decoration, all the others were soon using that new method or something very like it. Whether an idea was copied, swapped or sold is not known. All the big firms had much the same degree of technical proficiency and the only significant difference in the tiles was in the design and method of decoration. There are exceptions but the differences are very minor.*

The method of producing wall tiles, as Prosser and Minton had developed it, changed little, if at all, throughout the century. The only other important change was the invention of the steam-driven press,

* Sherwin & Cotton (established 1877), for instance, developed a Patent Lock Back: two recesses were undercut on the back of the tile to give a more effective grip for fixing.

which was first used by Maw & Co. in 1873. This machine did not alter the character of the tiles but it could produce them more quickly and with less manpower. A piston, with a vertical pressure of eighty tons, dropped on to the mould, stamped the tile and withdrew. C. T. Davis, writing about American tiles in 1895, said that the steam press could make tiles so quickly that he hardly had time to put one on the stack before another was handed to him. By this time the layout of the pottery was substantially different and everything was arranged to facilitate the speed of production. In 1883, Maw & Co. moved to new and larger premises in Jackfield and a great deal of care went into the design of the place: gravity feeds brought the clay dust down from the floor above, for instance, in order that the working floor should not be encumbered with more carts and trollies than was necessary.

All the developments of the nineteenth century that were related to the manufacture of the tile body were intended to speed up the process and increase production. Different methods of decoration (see chapter 5) could be worked at various speeds but the one aspect of production that invariably took time was the firing of the tiles. All kinds of pottery were fired in much the same way and the process changed very little, until the invention of the tunnel kiln just before the First World War. In America many of the kilns were fired by natural gas but the nineteenth-century English tile industry used local coal. The constant smoking from the kilns gave Stoke a characteristic and not very attractive atmosphere (plate 32). On a cloudy day, the smoke was held down over the towns and a yellow smog filled the streets. Arnold Bennett described the city as a 'desert of pot and cinders'. A character in *The Death of Simon Fuge*, with an apology for viewing it with the eyes of a 'clean-faced Southerner,' says that:

> It was squalid ugliness, but it was squalid ugliness on a scale that made it sublime. Great furnaces gleamed red in the twilight, and their fires were reflected in horrible black canals; processions of heavy vapours drifted in all directions across the sky, over what acres of miserable architecture! The air was alive with the most extraordinary, weird, gigantic sounds. I do not think the Five Towns will ever be described: Dante lived too soon.[20]

The old 'bottle-ovens' have disappeared from the Stoke skyline, but in the nineteenth century there were hundreds of them (plate 30), constantly belching out vast clouds of black smoke. In 1879, Minton, Hollins's had fourteen kilns at their premises in Shelton, New Road. They would have been fired in rotation so that some of them were being loaded or drawn throughout the week. The complete process took seven or eight days, depending on when it was started. If the oven was loaded on Saturday, a fairly slow, smoky fire was lit and the tiles dried and cured. Over the weekend the fire died down and on Monday it was rekindled and the heat gradually raised over the next two or three days, reaching a climax on Friday afternoon. The oven was left to cool during the following weekend and the contents were drawn on Tuesday morning. The ovens were literally bottle shaped and openings around the base gave access to several fires that fed into a central flue. Some twenty tons of coal were used for each firing. The tiles were placed over and around the fires in different positions according to their size and constitution. To avoid direct contact with the heat, they were stacked in 'saggars' (ceramic boxes) and these gave an even distribution of heat to their contents. This 'biscuit firing' had the highest temperature ($1160°C$; $2120°F$) and fixed the tile for size and shape. Small strips of tile were placed in pigeon holes, in various positions throughout the kiln and they could be withdrawn at any stage and examined. These trial pieces were the only clue as to what was going on inside once the door was closed.* They could be tested for colouring and dimension and relating to his experience the potter would know what stage had been reached. But firing was always a risky business and any small upset in the procedure could spoil the contents of the kiln.

Today, with modern industrial tile production, the efficiency of the manufacturing process can be reckoned in terms of the wastage, that is, the number of tiles that are rejected. They may fail to stand up to the strength test, there may be flaws in the glaze or an imperfection in the decoration. Altogether up to ten per cent of the tiles that leave the presses are rejected—and this is considered extremely efficient. A hundred years ago the wastage was much more than this and faults were very common (see Glossary *Faults* and plate 55). Even considering the most basic types of tile, one has to admire the skill and craft of the potter. Because we are so accustomed to the technical resources of the twentieth century, it is easy to forget the difficulties under which they worked in the last century. And, at the risk of overlooking some of the social aspects of the situation, admiration is in order. There was a fascination with the prospects of technical achievement. At best, their work represented a reconciliation between the Industrial Revolution and the creative instinct that was to be so self-consciously developed during the Art Movement. Without a doubt commercial interests were paramount in most cases; the working conditions were appalling by present day standards, silicosis and lead poisoning were rife. The blocks of old people's homes were a poor salve to the sores of exploitation. And yet, when the kiln was cool and the contents drawn, there must have been an air of excitement as the tiles were examined and the men could see the results of their labours.

* A kiln was fired to the verge of destruction and the temperature had to be carefully controlled. Inventions that helped to measure these high temperatures were directly linked to the work of the Stoke potters.

5 Decorative processes

Modern tile production has been so rationalized that only a very limited number of techniques are employed. But the Victorian potters had the benefit of a large, cheap labour force and if a new decorative process could be made to work in the kiln, it could be economically viable, even if much of the work had to be done by hand. It is often difficult to make clear distinctions between the many techniques employed: similar effects could be produced in a variety of ways and a slight alteration in the chemistry of the colours or the temperature of the firing completely changed the result. Once the biscuit was made it was quite common for several different processes to be used in the decoration of one tile: for instance, a transfer-printed tile might have a pattern that was filled in by hand; further colouring might then be applied on top of the glaze.

Many subtle and complicated techniques were devised for decorating tiles, but they were not commonly used. The basic methods of decoration were as follows:

Encaustic decoration
Encaustic tiles, by definition, had a clay pattern embedded into the body of the tile. The two sections were fused together during firing. The indentations in the slab were filled with coloured slips (which had the consistency of treacle) or dust clay. The composition of the filling material would produce different colours (plate 6).

Plain glazes
A glaze is essentially a coating applied to the tile that gives it a hard smooth surface; it may be clear or coloured, transparent or opaque. White lead, flint, stone and china clay were ground to form a glaze base and then finely ground metallic oxides were added to give the colours required. This compound was pan-ground in water to a fine suspended solution. The biscuit, which could be plain or embossed, was dipped by hand into a bowl of this glaze and then fired in a glost kiln at a temperature of about 1020°C (1870°F). A clear glaze brought out the colour of the body whether it was white, grey, red or brown and might be applied over any coloured decoration given to the tile such as a transfer print. 'Inglaze' colours, that is, stains mixed with the glaze, were formed by the addition of various chemicals; cobalt gave blue, for instance, or copper oxide was used for green. An opaque glaze was obtained by using tin oxide in the base. Striking effects could be achieved by applying coloured glaze to an embossed tile. When the dry biscuit was dipped into the glaze the water soaked in almost immediately, leaving a deposit on the surface. This became fluid during the firing and ran into the hollows of the relief pattern. A deeper colour formed where the glaze was thickest. Occasionally it is possible to see

how the glaze has flowed to one side of the tile because it was not set perfectly horizontal in the kiln (plate 55). Several colours could be used in one tile by 'floating in' the glazes with a brush. The contours of the pattern retained the colours or they could be allowed to flow together across the tile (plates 36 and 37).

Hand-painting

Using specially prepared colours the artist painted freely on to a tile (or set of tiles) that had a plain smooth surface. Once the technique was mastered it was similar to using watercolours but the effect was never certain until after the tiles had been fired and so it required great expertise to know how the colours would match together. The painting was usually done on a white biscuit and after being decorated a clear glaze was applied. In some cases the design was drawn freehand though it was often copied from an original sketch, using a technique called 'pouncing'. The main lines of the pattern were pricked through a sheet of paper and charcoal dusted through the holes on to the surface of the tile. A rough outline of the design could then be followed by the artist, ensuring a reasonable accuracy when several tiles were made from one original. This was a traditional technique used for the old Delft tiles and William De Morgan reproduced many of his designs in this way. An alternative method for copying an outline was to use a transfer pattern that could be filled in by hand. Although this was more accurate it was argued that the individuality and expressiveness of the design was lost. Hand-painted tiles of this sort are usually easy to recognize because of the range of colours and tones that were used (plate 29).

Pâte sur pâte

Great skill and accuracy were required for work of this sort and examples are not very common. A slight relief was built up over a dark ground by applying a large number of thin coats of white slip. Contrast was created according to the thickness of the slip in different parts of the image. It was a lengthy and painstaking process and few people were competent to work in this medium. In a debased form it was sometimes used to highlight parts of a design, often a transfer print. Where it has been used in this way, to throw into relief a mountain or the petals of a flower, it can be detected by passing a finger across the surface of the tile: the unevenness can always be felt (plate 39).

Sgraffito

Many of the very earliest tiles were decorated using this process. It is also the easiest way of marking a pattern on to a tile. The body of the tile is covered with one or more coats of slip and when dried the design is scratched into the coating, revealing the colour of the body beneath (plate 38).

Tube-lining

This technique was often used for mural work when areas of different colours were separated by small raised seams of clay, squeezed on to the tile like sugar icing. Opaque or transparent glazes were then welled into the design and the technique was rather like a 'painting by numbers' picture. The design was often marked out by pouncing. On individual tiles the effect is little different from that of an embossed tile which could be stamped to the same design (plate 51).

Transfer printing
The vast majority of tiles were transfer printed and were often subsequently filled-in by hand. The design was printed on to a tissue-paper transfer in a variety of colours, using engraved or etched plates. The tissue was first cut to shape and sized on one side with a special paste. The ink was prepared using powdered colours mixed with oil. The tissue was then soaked, placed on top of the inked plate and passed through the rollers. The plate was then left by the fire to dry and the tissue later removed. The ink impression from the engraving remained glued to the paper, and the process could be repeated for each colour that was to be in the design. When the printing was complete a cutter trimmed the sheet and it was placed colour-side down on a biscuit fired tile. To ensure that the tissue stuck to the tile it was then rubbed gently before being soaked in water. The paper floated off the tile and the coloured transfer remained. After a low temperature firing to harden on the colours the decorated surface was coated with a clear glaze. Additional colouring might be done both over and under this glaze (plate 50).

Transfers printed by a lithographic process were made in the same way but flat areas of colour could be applied. The design was drawn or painted in wax on to a flat stone that received the ink from a roller. Outlines were less accurate but for broad areas of colour the process was more effective than hand-painting because of the evenness of the impression (plate 9).

Aerography
This technique was not commonly used for decorating ceramic tiles, although the technique has many advantages. Work done in this way can be identified on close examination: specks of colour, like fine stipple, can be seen. Using a stencil, the process was very quick and an even coating of colour could be applied (plates 48 and 49).

The skills involved in decorating tiles were even greater than the complexities of making the tile body. The chemistry of glazes was always uncertain. Alumina, boracic acid, borax soda, nitre, pearlash, zinc and tin oxides, iron compounds, manganese, cobalt, nickel, copper or chromium, might be combined in different proportions to produce different effects. Each potter had a secret book of recipes that specified the ingredients, how they should be ground and mixed and to what consistencies. It can never be said that the potter's art was mechanical. A glaze reacted differently according to the composition of the tile body and different firing temperatures; the different glazes on two tiles might react with one another in the kiln, the heat acting as a catalyst; discrepancies in colour and tone might occur in two different mixes, even when the ingredients were the same. There was the problem of temperature control and firing: it was important to have an even temperature throughout the kiln and it is sometimes possible to see the minor variations within one tile where one side was hotter than the other.

No tile could be made with less than two firings: one for the biscuit and the second for the glaze. Close examination of a tile, however, may reveal that it was fired as many as four times. For instance, it might first be biscuit fired, then be given a transfer decoration which would need to be hardened on; a coat of glaze would then be applied and fired and further decoration, to highlight the design, might be painted overglaze. The tile would then be fired for the fourth time in an enamel kiln, to a lower temperature (about 750°C; 1380°F), to fix the final colours without allowing the glaze to run. Overglaze decoration can sometimes be detected by looking at the tile from an angle: parts of the design appear to float above the body since there is the thickness of the glaze in between; it may also appear relatively matt in certain lights.

In the fifties, when Arnoux was doing so much of the pioneering work at Minton's, the colours and glazes were prepared at the pottery. Twenty years later, when tile making became a big business, a new trade was established which supplied to the manufacturers all the raw materials required. A typical firm of this sort was started in about 1870 by A. F. Wenger. From his premises in Etruria (Staffordshire) Wenger supplied potters throughout the world with his own ready-mixed colours and glazes. Even William De Morgan is known to have experimented with Wenger's glazes. A catalogue offered hundreds of different colours for under- and overglaze painting. Some of them, particularly a range of purples and blues, were marked 'flowing': that is to say, they were non-refractory and would flow into the glaze at a relatively low temperature. There was an important distinction made between under- and overglaze colours, which developed differently when fired.

Wenger's also sold a full range of utensils and tools for the potters' work, from saggars down to pallette knives. The business was a natural response to an expanding industry. Few of the tile manu-facturers were big enough to employ their own chemists, so firms like Wenger's practically provided a 'do-it-yourself' potters' kit. As a result there was a rapid increase in the number of firms working, not as manufacturers, but as art tile decorators. This development coincided with the Aesthetic Movement and these decorators self-consciously pursued Art and Beauty in their designs. The firm of W. B. Simpson and Sons has been mentioned in this connection and Carter and Co. (established 1873) were working in a similar vein. Minton's Art Pottery Studios in Kensington Gore, London, which were opened in 1871, employed many artists (and would-be artists) to decorate their products which were sent down, biscuit fired, from Stoke. These painters, while skilful and dextrous with a brush, probably knew little or nothing about the chemistry of glazes and it is safe to assume that they were supplied with ready-made colours, quite possibly by Wenger's.

As the ancillary supply trades grew up around the Potteries, the manufacturers were able to concentrate more on the production of the actual tiles. Some firms specialized in making dies and others in engraving copper plates. It seems likely that a number of printers were also engaged to supply completed transfers. In 1848, Herbert Minton held a patent with Messrs Collins and Reynolds; they had sent him the results of their experiments in printing for tiles and the process was developed mutually. But it is difficult to imagine that, in later years, each pottery had its own department making printed transfers. In any business as trade expands it opens up the possibility for other firms to supply materials. Then, if one manufacturer begins to dominate the market (as has happened in tile production this century), it becomes large enough to warrant expenditure on plant and equipment to process raw materials within the company or group. This then leads to the inevitable decline of the supply trades.

Firms like Wenger's made an important contribution to the growth of the industry. Just as the dust-press assisted mass-production, so prepared materials assisted mass-decoration. By 1880 one of the most severe problems facing the tile manufacturers was the difficulty of producing the goods fast enough. Solon's *pâte sur pâte* panels of chained cupids and forlorn maidens (plate 39), were technically skilful but expensive in terms of time and materials. They should be seen in contrast to the well designed transfer-printed tiles (plate 45) which were easier to make and could be rapidly produced in large numbers. It is interesting to note that Wedgwood's, who made many more tiles than is generally realized, used transfer printing on almost all of them. The best known designs, like the series of months, the twelve *Midsummer Night's Dream* designs and the six tiles telling the story of Little Red Riding Hood, were usually one-colour transfer prints.* They used dust-pressed tiles, many of which are unmarked and may possibly have been made by another firm. Copeland's on the other hand, used handmade plastic clay tiles, almost exclusively. But they too made extensive use of transfers and the company still have a complete set of copper plates that were used for the eight-inch tiles illustrating the months of the year. In their case, only the outline was printed and in the pattern books, that recorded every tile that they made, there are instructions as to the colour mixes to be used for filling in the design.

The most successful nineteenth-century tiles were those that best employed the skills and qualities of the medium. They had to be made from compressed clay dust: any other method was not economical by comparison. To exploit the quality of tiles and their suitability as a decorative wall covering, a repeating pattern was best—if well designed it could be extended over any surface. But transfer prints were not substantially different from any other printed work: the surface could

* The months of the year were also produced as polychrome designs.

as well be wallpaper. A good transfer-printed design should also relate to the six-inch units, but it does not have the depth and tone in the glaze that other processes achieve—the surface is always flat and the pattern superficial. Embossed tiles with one or more transparent colour glazes (plates 27 and 36) utilize the possibility of shaping the surface of the tile body—a process that can be effected at no extra expense in time or money. The embossed majolica tiles might be considered the most satisfactory examples of industrial tile production; and certainly after 1900 the majority were manufactured in this way.

There were two other techniques of decoration that deserve special mention. Lustre ware was produced in the nineties by a few firms such as Maw's and J. C. Edwards. Its introduction for tile decoration was almost entirely a result of De Morgan's work in this medium. The distinguishing factor in the production of lustre ware (plate 54) is that the tiles are briefly fired in a reducing atmosphere (usually coal gas) which breaks down the copper oxide on the tile. The tile was fired normally in the oven, at a temperature of about 700 °C (1290 °F). At a certain stage the gas was pumped in and allowed to burn from the top of the chimney. Why the whole place did not explode nobody could quite decide! After about five minutes the gas tap was turned off and the top of the kiln plugged, leaving the gas-filled oven to work its spell of chemistry. The firing was done in an enamel kiln after the tile had already been fired in the glost kiln to develop the copper glaze. On going into the oven the tile would have been the bright green colour that is normally associated with copper. It was a delicate process since copper is highly reactive as a glaze and the slightest overfiring would burn away the lustre, leaving a rather flat, murky red colour instead of the irides-cent sheen that is proper to this kind of decoration.

In the nineties Sherwin and Cotton developed a clever process that employed photography to reproduce life-like impressions of people and scenes by forming a subtly moulded relief beneath the glaze (plate 52). Leading men of the day were captured in ceramic. But, although these tiles were made in quite large numbers and are amusing items to collect, they are not typical of the main stream of tile production.

It has already been suggested that six-inch wall tiles were particularly suited to machine production. They were often used to decorate large areas of a wall with a repeating pattern. Here, the machine was particu-larly applicable, because it could accurately multiply the individual motif and extend it across a plane with vertical, horizontal and diagonal links in the pattern. These tiles required as much skill, care and expertise as hand-painted designs. The process was no less difficult and the work of the designer no less exacting. In fact it is probably easier to draw a design for an individual tile, for instance the Copeland tiles (plate 29), than it is to devise a pattern that will stand up to repetition, such as the panel made by Maw & Co. (plate 83), a typical product of the machine. The outlines of the Copeland tiles were printed from copper plates and the colours filled in by hand; the tiles were probably made for a music room and might have been set into the wall to relieve a plain glaze tile surface. Alternatively, they might have been set into the back of a piece of furniture, a wash-stand, sideboard or mantelpiece. In any case, they were intended to be seen individually, as parts of a matching set. The images have charm and humour: the medieval instrumentalists, watched over by sunflowers, are thoroughly in keeping with the mood of the 1870s. The designs are attractive, but not particularly suited to tiles—they could as easily have been paintings or cartoons in a music book. On the other hand, the intersecting circles of the extending pattern in the Maw design, the depth and subtlety of the glazes, the contrasts of colour and shapes—everything adds up to the most perfect production of ceramic tiles. The tiles were made in imitation of Moorish designs and demonstrate the considerable expertise that Maw's achieved in this kind of work. But they were made by machine and mass-produced.

Machine-made tiles were cheaper, simpler, and made in larger numbers but that should not detract from their quality and value. Most of Moyr Smith's designs for Minton's were transfer printed (plate 86); the famous Wedgwood tiles illustrating the months of the year were transfer printed and so were Kate Greenaway's seasons, made by T. & R. Boote (plate 87). None of Morris's or De Morgan's designs were transfers and they are no better for that fact. The quality of the product depended on how well it was done, rather than on how it was done. But the machine was blamed for any bad decorative design.

At the turn of the century people were beginning to see the need to revise some established ideas about the arts and crafts. If decorated tiles were to be supplied for the popular market, then it was necessary to accept the use of machinery. The quality of the product would depend on the quality of the design. Furnival, in his book *Leadless Decorative Tiles, Faience and Mosaics*, remarks that:

> Hyper-critical minds have questioned the artistic bearing of the extensive use of mechanical means of decoration, but it must be confessed that reproduction of designs suffused with genuine artistic feeling and skill are more likely to yield permanent pleasure than hand-painted perpetrations of mediocrity. There is a case in point in the old Delft tiles; so long as they were decorated by clever artists, all was well, but when decadence set in the results were pitiably inferior.[21]

Joseph Chamberlain (The Right Honourable) wrote in 1899 that 'we must recognize the necessity for seeking the assistance of machinery and of all devices which would bring within the reach of many, if not the highest works of art, at all events something elevated and something which might be accepted as a provisional substitute.'[22] How far the machine was a substitute for manual work, in the context of art and design, had always been a matter for debate.

6 The American art tile companies

In 1895, C. T. Davis[23] remarked that, although there were no tiles at all manufactured in America 'a few years ago', it was by then a thriving industry with thousands of dollars invested; the demand was greater than the supply from home and abroad. Although it is true that a considerable number of companies were established in the last two decades of the century, in fact only a handful of them were to be constantly in production for more than a few years. One of the most characteristic qualities of the American tile industry, in the 1880s and 1890s, was the rapid succession of names that drifted through the records. Nearly thirty companies are known to have been established before 1900, but very few survived. Nonetheless, the production of tiles in the United States was sufficient to depress the British export trade quite considerably. The American art tile manufacturers showed great initiative and originality—their development warrants full consideration in the history of nineteenth-century tiles.

Early transfer-printed tiles, made by Sadler and Green, of Liverpool, were shipped to America in large numbers during the eighteenth century. They were used extensively as fireplace facings in the colonial homes of the pre-revolutionary era. Examples of such work can be seen in the Henry Wadsworth Longfellow House, in Cambridge, Mass., the Jeremiah Lee House, Marblehead, Mass., and in the Isaac Royall House, Medford, Mass. Although these tiles were popular and well received, there was little attempt to produce American tiles. In the nineteenth century, too, the English found a profitable export market in the States and many manufacturers established distributors to handle their business abroad. A typical agency of this sort was run by the Alfred Boote Co. in New York, which handled tiles of every description, made by Maw's; Miller, Coates & Youle handled imports from Minton, Hollins & Co., and Conover & Co. managed the affairs of Brown's of Paisley and the Campbell Brick & Tile Co. These early contractors were principally dealers in mantelpieces, fireplaces and stoves, selling imported tiles for hearths and grate-linings. In those days, a tiled bathroom was a curiosity and was installed only in very wealthy homes. But the command that the English manufacturers had over the market, in the seventies, was soon to be challenged by the American potters.

The Centennial Exposition, held in Philadelphia in 1876, inspired a new enthusiasm for art and industry and the 'art industries'. There had been other international exhibitions in America. In 1853, for instance, the 'World of Science, Art and Industry' was held at the Crystal Palace, New York. Among the English exhibitors, Minton's had an extensive display of encaustic and majolica tiles. But more significant to the growth of the American industry were the ten-inch tiles that floored the stand of the United States Pottery of Bennington, Vermont. With a white body and inlaid with colours, the tiles were designed with an ornamental centre-piece and a border with the American flag in each corner. The problems of further production proved too much for the firm, however, and they did not pursue this work. Abraham Miller is said to have made some tiles at an even earlier date, at his factory in Philadelphia. Apparently he used large panels (18 × 12 in.) to face his warehouse and also made some ceramic slabs for the terrace of his house.

Samuel Keyes is considered to be the first man to have had any success with tiles. He was an Englishman by birth, and while manager of the brickworks at Pittsburgh he began experiments with the manufacture of floor tiles. He started in 1867 and within four years was making encaustic tiles successfully. In 1876, he was superintendent of the Pittsburgh Encaustic Tile Co., which was reorganized six years later as the Star Encaustic Tiling Co. It is not known whether Samuel Keyes exhibited his work at Philadelphia in 1876. But there were certainly some elaborate displays brought over from England. Tiles were becoming very fashionable in Britain by this time and the European manufacturers were keen to establish themselves in America, which offered such a large market for export. Ironically their efforts also stimulated the growth of the American tile industry. The 1876 exhibition was a large one by any standards. With seventy-five acres of buildings and twenty-five miles of avenues and walks, tourists were advised to allow three days to look round the site. Among the visitors were several men who were shortly to set up their own potteries and begin to manufacture American ceramics.

The Philadelphia Exposition was perfectly timed to counteract the aftermath of the American Civil War. After any war there tends to be a national reaction, which often takes the form of a romantic yearning for the simplicity of a quiet farming life. With the growth of the Art Movement, at this time in the nineteenth century, the perfect symbol for peace and prosperity was to be found in the aesthetics of 'good taste' and the refinements of manufactured art. *The Artist and Journal of Home Culture* was, therefore, pleased to report on 'a recent remarkable growth of the pottery industry in the United States, chiefly in New York and New Jersey [which] may, not unnaturally, cause some anxiety in the potteries at home. Trenton in the last named State, is now the acknowledged centre of a manufacture which, so recently as a quarter of a century since had not extended beyond the most insignificant proportions. The New Jerseyites are boasting that ere long their productiveness in fictile ware will practically enable them to defy and shut out all foreign competition.'[24] By 1880, there were twenty potteries in Trenton alone and 104 in the whole of America. Many of them were producing tiles.

In the 1880s, 'estheticism' [sic] was the rage. Oscar Wilde had given his celebrated tour of lectures and even if Americans found his pose and affectation rather distasteful, there was a wide response to the ideas that he was propagating. It was in this context that the 'art tile' became so popular. Caryl Coleman wrote a series of articles on the history of tiles in *The Decorator and Furnisher* and points to modern tiles as the perfect material for refined decoration:

> The day is not far distant when stoves in this country will be made entirely of tiles and the frightful nickel-plated iron monsters, so ugly in form and weak beyond expression in ornament, will be banished forever from our homes . . . Stoves with us now are in the transition stage, the struggle between iron and earthenware has begun, between the commonplace and the artistic, between the cheap and the ornate.[25]

The designs of many of the tiles made for stoves of this sort were extremely sentimental by today's standard. A tile in high relief, made by Low's and entitled 'Flying Moments', pictured 'a beautiful conceit . . . in which three Cupids hover around an hour-glass, one being depicted in the act of winging his way upwards'.[26] The subject is reminiscent of some of M. L. Solon's work for Minton's, of about the same period.

The Aesthetic Movement in England encouraged many oddities and bizarre fashions, but in America aestheticism was treated in a forthright and direct way:

> The love of beauty finds a place in every refined mind and is a germ that desires cultivation, and is ever on the lookout for means of gratifying that desire; strip estheticism of its habilement of charlatanism, its 'vague platitudes', its lackadaisical airs and graces—of all that is unmanly—return it to its original and true principles and we find it simply a true and healthy yearning for higher knowledge and culture; a seeking to surround the home and everyday life with objects of true beauty, to fill the mind with higher thoughts, with soft refining influences that may lift us out of the narrow sphere into which the prosaic duties of everyday life—sometimes in spite of ourselves—induce us; a home governed by such influences, is, to those associated with it, like the cheerful sunshine breaking through the clouds of commonplace life, and flooding it with new and subtle influences and pleasures, never to be forgotten, as long as life lasts: thus estheticism, robbed of its outward show and supercilious gloss, may be brought to bear upon our homes and lives with good refining influence, without reproach, or fear of adverse criticism.[27]

There is no evasion here. What was wanted was something that could be called 'truly beautiful'. Many of the decorative tiles made in America were intended to be just that and although it may be difficult to stomach the extravagance of the nineteenth-century journalists, it is true that the best work has a natural delicacy that is very appealing.

One of the best known manufacturers of such tiles was the firm of J. & J. G. Low, of the Art Tile Works, Chelsea, Mass. Mr John Gardner

Low, who founded the company, was born in Chelsea, 1835. He studied painting and drawing as a young man and spent some time in Paris. Not long after he returned to America, he went to work with the Robertson family at a small pottery in his home town. These were the same Robertsons who later established the Robertson Art Tile Co., in Morrisville. It was James Robertson, who taught Low his trade and in the early seventies he worked chiefly on imitation Greek pots. One authority mentions that 'George W. Robertson, in 1872, was the first to make pressed-clay dust tiles in this country and tiles were made by James Robertson as early as 1860.'[28] This is not substantiated by any other writer. In 1877, Low went into business on his own account and with his father Mr John Low (a civil engineer) he set up a pottery for making tiles. It was, undoubtedly, the Centennial Exposition which inspired this move. The works stood at 948 Broadway, on the corner of Stockton Street (plate 31). There was considerable delay before the business was operational—it was intended from the outset that the company should manufacture tiles on a large scale and it took time to organize the venture. The first firing took place on 1 May 1879. Within five months Low had won a silver medal at the Cincinnati Exposition. The future looked bright.

It was not long before the firm was invited to display tiles in England, at an exhibition organized by the Royal Manchester, Liverpool and North Lancashire Agricultural Society. In competition with experienced English manufacturers, Low's won the Gold Medal. As well as personal triumph, his success demonstrated the rapid development of which the American tile industry was capable. Low had little or no experience of tile production and his work was based on his own experiments. He developed a unique method of decoration that was patented under the name of the 'natural process'. In 1882, the firm had an exhibition of work at the Fine Arts Society, in New Bond Street, London. The *Pall Mall Gazette* described the tiles as 'a fresh departure' and the *London Court Journal* noted that 'this gentleman has invented a new species of Keramic ware. The first that America has produced in any high order.'

Instead of painting or printing a picture on the surface of the biscuit, which was likely to be no more than a colourful imitation, Low used the natural object itself. 'How did I first think of that?' he said:

> I was bothering over a dust tile and this process is a half-century old, and ought not to bother anyone—when suddenly it occurred to me that it might be possible to stamp a figure or a letter, or indeed, any form whatever, upon the face of the tile, just as the manufacturer's name is stamped upon the back . . . I naturally thought of leaves as the material nearest at hand, and rushing out of the shop, down behind there, towards the brickyard, I found a mullein-leaf. I hurried back, put the dust into the press, flattened it down by a light pressure of the screw, then laying on the leaf, gave the screw a hard turn. I pressed the juice all out of the leaf, but I got my imprint perfectly,

ribs and all, even to the downy texture of the surface. This was not such a startling success, but I was in a fever of excitement and anxiety over my experiments and at the sight of the imprint of the mullein-leaf, went fairly out of my head with delight. I kept at the work all night long, trying many sorts of leaves, grass and various combinations. The next day I went on with the experiments and the day after and the day after that and at last made perfect patterns of leaves and grass. Having made the matrix, it was now the problem to make the die from it, for the tile ought to bear the pattern in relief . . . [After making experiments] I tried fine Japanese paper and finally came to use tissue paper, as you can see.[29]

Over the first impression, a thin tissue was laid and a second tile pressed, as it were from a mould. Thus there were two copies taken: a male and a female of the same design. These tiles could then be glazed and fired, as normal. 'I call these *natural tiles*', Low goes on to say, 'and the process is patented; the beauty of it is that we never make two originals exactly alike in composition.' The technique might have seemed unethical to many English designers, but the result was refreshingly simple and attractive (plate 97).

This was not Low's only contribution to the art of tile making. The firm produced a wide variety of designs and specialized, among other things, in 'art tile soda fountains'. This was a field peculiar to the Americans, although Minton, Hollins's did similar work for the World's Fair at St Louis (1904). Almost the entire range of Low's tiles can be seen in their *Illustrated Catalogue of Art Tiles Made by J. G. & J. F. Low*, published in 1884.* (John Low, the father, had retired from the firm in 1883 and John Gardiner Low was now in partnership with his son, John F.—hence J. G. & J. F. Low.) As well as the 'natural process' tiles, there were series of panels with idealized portraits and mythical heads. More life-like images included tiles featuring famous American Presidents such as Cleveland, Lincoln and Grant. And some of the most notable pieces done by the firm were the 'plastic sketches' or 'poems in clay' designed and modelled by Arthur Osborne.

Osborne trained in England and had joined the Low family at the start of the venture. The natural process, which established the firm's early reputation, was to become less important in later years and Osborne's moulded plaques formed the major part of the pottery's output. They were made up to two feet in length and cast from plaster moulds. The original was sculpted in low relief, working directly in plastic clay and from this a plaster of paris mould was made. Each copy was then formed by rolling out clay, rather like pastry and forcing it, by hand, into the pattern. After a brief period of drying, the cast was removed and the new tile was reworked by hand. This involved undercutting parts of the design, a process that gave greater depth to

* A copy of the catalogue can be seen at the Massachusetts Institute of Technology and the Cooper Hewitt Museum of Decorative Arts.

65 Morris & Co., *c.* 1872; two tiles with hand-painted designs probably by Burne-Jones. The
firm made relatively few tiles and after about 1875 made use of De Morgan's work in
their schemes for interior decoration. Victoria & Albert Museum, London.

66 Della Robbia Co., *c.* 1895; plaque moulded from plastic clay with pale green and
yellow glazes. By permission City Museum, Stoke-on-Trent.

67 Minton's China Works, *c.* 1875; a pair of finely painted tiles by a Japanese artist, 8 in. (signed on the back).

68 Campbell Brick & Tile Co., *c.* 1875; three of a set of five hand-painted tiles. The influence of the Japanese taste is evident in these delicately painted designs, here modified by an English artist.

69 No marks, *c.* 1875; one of a pair of tiles with a hand-painted design on a grey ground, 12 x 6 in. Sotheby & Co., London.

70 J. & J. G. Low, plaque by Arthur Osborne, 24 x 8 in. Smithsonian Institution, Washington DC.

71 J. & J. G. Low, *c.* 1885; a green-tan plaque modelled by Arthur Osborne, 15 x 8 in. Smithsonian Institution, Washington DC.

69

70

71

72 Cambridge Art Tile Works, *c.* 1895; two tiles, 18 x 6 in., in dark brown, representing night and morning. They are very similar to some tiles (plate 73) by the English firm of Gibbons, Hinton & Co. Smithsonian Institution, Washington DC.

73 Gibbons, Hinton & Co. *c.* 1895; majolica tile, 16 x 6 in. Probably part of a set (morning, noon and night) with various coloured glazes; this one is brown.

ASTE NOT

ANT NOT

A PLACE
FOR EVERYTHING
AND EVERYTHING
IN ITS
PLACE

74 *top left and right*: Minton & Co., *c.* 1850; early dust-pressed tiles (marked 'Prossers Patent' on the back). Such Victorian homilies reminded kitchen-girls of their responsibilities. *top middle*: no marks, black transfer print of Conway Castle. *middle left*: Maw & Co.; brown transfer print with Japanese design. Collection Ian Craig. *middle*: Wedgwood, one of a set of twelve illustrations to *Midsummer Night's Dream*; brown transfer print. Collection Ian Craig. *middle right*: Wedgwood, the month of May: brown transfer print. Collection Ian Craig. *bottom left*: no marks, Invergarry Castle; polychrome transfer print. One of a series of views of Scottish castles. *bottom middle*: Minton's China Works, *c.* 1880; buff body with black transfer print. One of a set of twenty-four Shakespeare designs by J. Moyr Smith. The same designs were also printed in blue and brown. *bottom right*: 'L & D', *c.* 1895; polychrome transfer. Redvers Buller was one of the more incompetent British Generals in the Boer War. Collection Ian Craig.

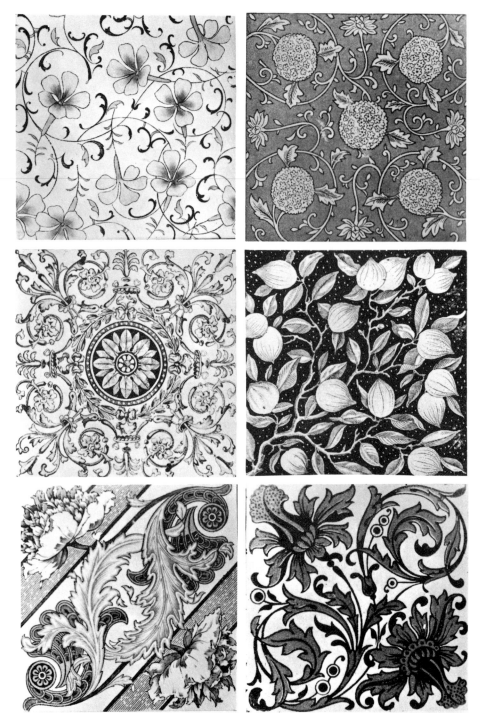

75. *top left*: Minton's China Works, *c.* 1900; brown transfer print with pink flowers. *top right*: Minton's China Works, brown transfer print on buff body. Collection H. & R. Johnson-Richards. *middle left*: Minton, Hollins & Co., 1888; two-tone transfer print. Collection H. & R. Johnson-Richards. *middle right*: Maw & Co., *c.* 1880; blue litho-printed transfer. Collection H. & R. Johnson-Richards. *bottom left*: Wedgwood, two-tone blue transfer. Collection H. & R. Johnson-Richards. *bottom right*: Maw & Co., *c.* 1895; two-tone brown litho-printed transfer. By permission Susan Ford.

76 *top left*: no marks, *c.* 1895; hand-painted polychrome design. *top middle*: Minton, Hollins & Co., blue, pink, green and white. By permission City Museum, Stoke-on-Trent. *top right*: Minton, 1875; 10 in. hand-painted in blue by M. E. Black. One of many tiles forming a dado in the old Grill Room at the Victoria & Albert Museum (plate 100). By permission Victoria & Albert Museum, London. *middle left*: Maw & Co., *c.* 1880; 'anglo-persian' design in blue, green, brown, purple and orange. Collection H. & R. Johnson-Richards. *middle*: Minton & Co., *c.* 1860; majolica tile in blue, yellow, cherry and white from Crewe Hall. Collection H. & R. Johnson-Richards. *middle right*: Maw & Co., *c.* 1880; blue majolica tile. The same design is illustrated in the firm's catalogue (plate 27). Collection H. & R. Johnson-Richards. *bottom left*: Campbell Brick and Tile Co., *c.* 1895; 8. in. majolica tile with brown glaze. *bottom middle*: Minton, 1872; 8 in. majolica tile in blues, yellow, green and brown. The rebated edges suggest that the tile was made for a window-box. *bottom right*: Minton, Hollins & Co., 8 in. majolica tile with red border, yellow, green, grey and black decoration. Collection H. & R. Johnson-Richards.

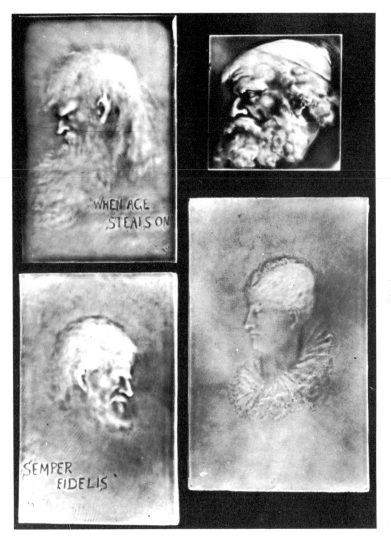

77 J. & J. G. Low, Arthur Osborne designs: *top left*: 'When Age Steels On', yellow-green *c.* 1885, 7x11 in. *top right*: bearded man, yellow-brown 1881, 6 in. *bottom left*: 'Semper Fidelis', yellow-green *c.* 1885, 7 x 11 in. *bottom right*: head of a woman, yellow-green *c.* 1885, 13 x 8 in. Smithsonian Institution, Washington DC.

78 Cambridge Art Tile Works, *c.* 1890; light green plaque, 18 x 6 in., depicting 'Poetry' in a style rather similar to some of Solon's work at Minton's China Works. Smithsonian Institution, Washington DC.

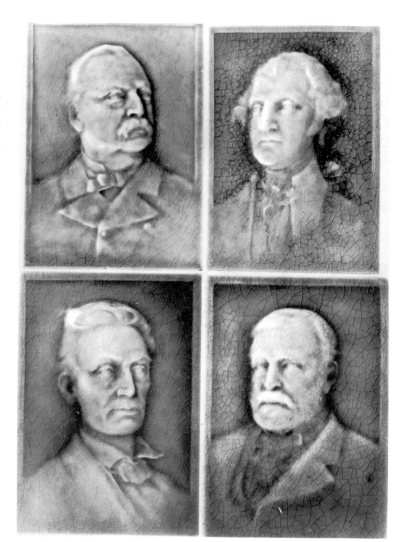

79 J. & J. G. Low, 1885, portraits of American Presidents, Lincoln, Washington, Cleveland and Grant. Smithsonian Institution, Washington DC.

80 Trent Tile Co., head of Michelangelo in amber glaze *c.* 1890. Smithsonian Institution, Washington DC.

81 J. & J. G. Low, *c.* 1885; yellow-brown tile in original iron frame, 10¼ in. Smithsonian Institution, Washington DC.

80 81

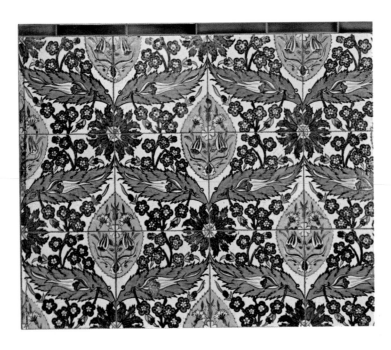

82 Maw & Co., *c.* 1880 (a copy of an 'Isnik' design *c.* 1570); transfer pattern filled-in by hand. Collection H. & R. Johnson-Richards.

83 Maw & Co., *c.* 1880; fine majolica tiles pressed from dust clay; the relief pattern and the richly coloured glazes make full use of the medium. Collection H. & R. Johnson-Richards.

Opposite
84 Maw & Co., *c.* 1880; transfer printed design. Collection H. & R. Johnson Richards.

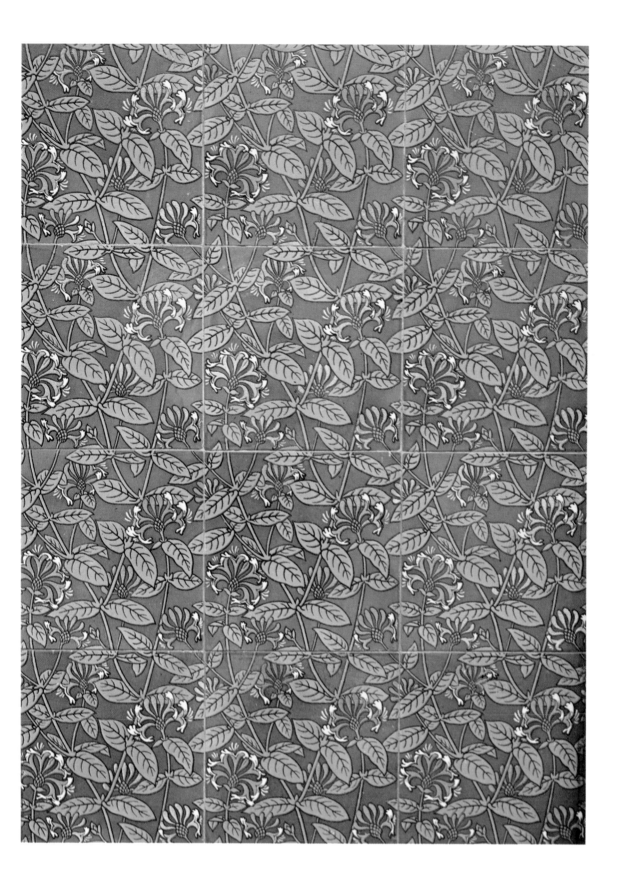

85 Minton, Hollins & Co., *c.* 1890; January and May from the months of the year. Black and red litho-printed transfers, 8 in. By permission Richard Dennis.

86 Minton's China Works, *c.* 1885; four from a set of twelve 'Seasons' designed by J. Moyr Smith. Four-colour transfer prints. Collection H. & R. Johnson-Richards.

87 T. & R. Boote, 1881; three of the seasons designed by Kate Greenaway. Pink transfer
pattern, central section hand-coloured. By permission Victoria & Albert Museum,
London.

88 Minton, Hollins & Co., *c.* 1880; brown body with hand-painted design in natural
colour, blue pot with ochre base. Collection H. & R. Johnson-Richards.

89 *top left*: Copeland, c. 1875; 8 in. biscuit made from plastic clay with pattern in orange, green and gold. By permission City Museum, Stoke-on-Trent. *top right*: Copeland, 1850, 8 in. biscuit made from plastic clay with black transfer pattern hand-coloured in green, yellow, pink and blue. *bottom left*: Minton, Hollins & Co., two-tone blue litho-printed transfer pattern; 8 in. Collection H. & R. Johnson-Richards. *bottom right*: no marks, polychrome litho-printed transfer pattern. Collection H. & R. Johnson-Richards.

90 *top left:* Craven Dunnill, grey litho-printed transfer. Collection H. & R. Johnson-Richards. *top middle:* Malkin, Edge & Co., *c.* 1895; black transfer hand-coloured. Collection H. & R. Johnson-Richards. *top right:* Robert Minton Taylor, *c.* 1873; 4 in. neo-Delft hand-painted maroon design. Collection Ian Craig. *middle left:* Minton's China Works, brown body with hand-painted design in greys; 8 in. By permission Julie Hammond. *middle:* T. A. Simpson, 1881; hand-painted polychrome design predominantly brown with purple borders. Collection Ian Craig. *middle right:* Robert Minton Taylor, *c.* 1873; grey biscuit with overglaze painting in brown and white. Collection H. & R. Johnson-Richards. *bottom left:* Minton's China Works, *c.* 1885; one from a set illustrating *Aesop's Fables;* brown transfer-printed. Collection H. & R. Johnson-Richards. *bottom middle:* Minton, Hollins & Co., *c.* 1890; Abraham and Isaac, one of a series of Biblical subjects; decorated with an iridescent black glaze which gives prismatic colouring in certain lights. Collection H. & R. Johnson-Richards. *bottom right:* Copeland, 1880; 8 in. biscuit cut from plastic clay with polychrome hand-painted design, predominantly green border. Collection H. & R. Johnson-Richards.

91 Maw & Co., *c.* 1880; display panel from the Jackfield showroom. Collection H. & R. Johnson-Richards.

92 Maw & Co., *c.* 1880; panel of ecclesiastical tiles. Tiles were often used as commemorative plaques and elaborate designs such as this might be used for the reredos. Collection H. & R. Johnson-Richards.

93 Maw & Co., *c.* 1880; panel of tiles,
litho-printed transfer in greens, orange and white. Collection H. & R.
Johnson-Richards.

94 Maw & Co., *c.* 1880; display panel
from the Jackfield showroom. Collection H. & R. Johnson-Richards.

95 *top and bottom left*: C. Pardee Works, *c.* 1895; two 6 in. tiles with blue glaze depicting Grover Cleveland and James G. Blaine. *top right*: J. and J. G. Low, high relief flowers in deep green, 7½ in. *bottom right*: Robertson Art. Tile· Co., *c.* 1890; yellow brown. Smithsonian Institution, Washington DC.

op. Grueby Faience Co.,
. 1895; two tiles, winged
bull, green on blue
ground, and eagle, orange
on blue ground, 7½ in.
middle: Moravian Pot-
ery & Tile Works, *c.*
905; poorly modelled
relief tile in green,
brown, red, yellow and
black, 22 x 15 in. *bottom
left*: Batchelder, *c.* 1910;
Viking ship in brown on
blue, 4 in.
bottom right: Enfield
Pottery, *c.* 1907; duck in
brown on green. Smith-
onian Institution, Wa-
hington DC.

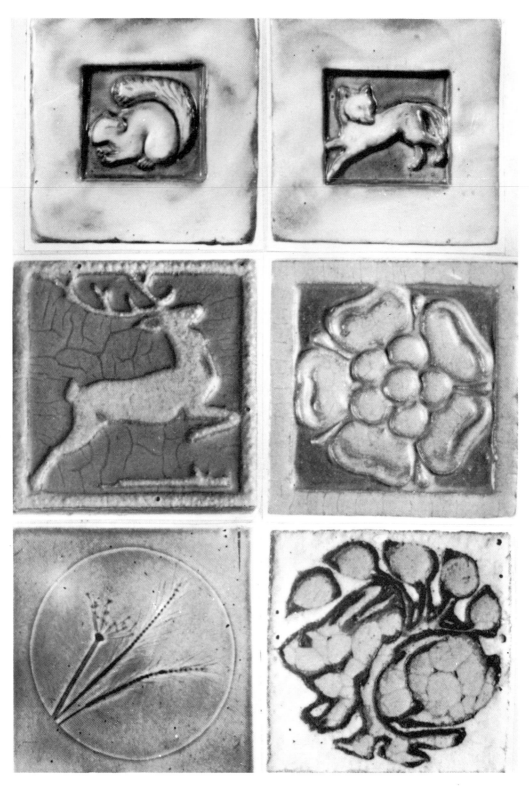

97 *top*: Moravian Pottery & Tile Works, *c.* 1895; two impressed tiles, yellow-green, 4 in. *middle*: Grueby Faience Co., *c.* 1895; two impressed tiles, 4 in. *bottom left*: Low's Art Tile Works, 1879-81; tile made by the 'natural' process. *bottom right*: Grueby Faience Co., *c.* 1895; stylized rabbit and plant, off-white and green, 4 in. Smithsonian Institution, Washington DC.

the portraits, landscapes and animal pictures, for which Osborne had such a reputation (plate 71). The farmyard scenes are particularly fine illustrations of rural life in New England.

Although Low's did not survive the depression in trade during the nineties, they probably made the greatest single contribution to the American art tile industry. As well as the initiative shown in the design of the tile, they experimented with new glazing techniques and produced results that were to give 'an entirely new value' to the established ideas of colour and texture. *Harper's Magazine* reported that 'by their process, tiles are not only modelled in relief, but are most beautifully graded in colour, a blush of a certain tone seeming to spread and deepen over the surface and while a certain grade of colour is adhered to in a number of tiles, no two are alike in the distribution of values and the surface is apparently a thin glaze overlying a molten depth.'[30] This could be done by a technique called 'clouding'. A spatula, with a piece of sponge attached to one end, was used to dab colour on to certain parts of the biscuit. The tile was then immediately dipped into the glaze so that the colours ran and spread across the face of the tile. The flow of the glaze was continued during firing, running into the depths of the design.

It is significant that the American manufacturers did not simply try to imitate the tiles exported from England, but concentrated on making tiles that were completely different in style and probably more suited to the home market. Davis, with a certain national pride, criticized the English industry for the sloppiness of its products, and his opinion accorded with many other critics at the end of the century. It is ironic, then, that so many of the leading figures in the American tile industry did in fact come from Britain. It was not until the end of the century that 'ceramic engineers' began to graduate from the American Universities. In 1896, the Ohio State University opened a course in ceramics, under the instruction of Edward Orton Jnr., and other establishments soon followed this lead. In the 1880s, however, there were very few American potters with any detailed knowledge of the technical aspects of tile-body mixes and the chemistry of glazes. The government was at pains to encourage the immigration of technicians who would aid the development of industry, rather than a rural population (like the victims of the Highland clearances) who would only add to the number of small-holdings. Even at this time, wages were reckoned to be one hundred per cent higher than in Europe and the opportunities that America offered persuaded many men to cross the Atlantic: their passports were the technicalities of their trades.

A tilewright whose career is typical was Fred H. Wilde who emigrated from England to America in 1885 and first went to work at the International Tile and Trim Co. in Brooklyn. This pottery had been organized some three years before, by John Ivory and his father. It was largely an English concern and received financial backing from 'the British aristocracy'. The factory was built on Third Street running through to Fourth, between Hoyt and Bond Streets. Mr Wilde himself recorded that most of the plant was imported: 'All the presses, dies and special machinery were brought from England. ·Many of the workers (all department heads) were brought over, including a printer and engraver.'[31] Wilde and many of the other men were from Maw's of Jackfield and, but for the inadequacy of the pottery itself, which was badly laid out, the company had every possible chance to succeed. However, the business suffered from successive changes in ownership and management (a very common problem in the early American tile industry); the English shareholders withdrew in 1886 and Wilde also soon left. Two years later a new company took over and until 1896 the business was run under the name of the New York Vitrified Tile Co. Mr A. H. Bonnell, who was then manager, bought the company and changed the name to the Brooklyn Vitrified Tile Works. Under this title it was to meet with considerable success, particularly in the floor tile and mosaic market. But, in 1906, the premises caught fire (this too was a common occurrence) and the entire plant was destroyed. After further mishaps, including the death of the proprietor and the financial panic of 1907, the pottery was rebuilt and business continued for another ten years, until nearly the end of the First World War. The early fortunes of this pottery are typical of those of many such companies of the period.

After leaving Brooklyn, Fred Wilde worked with the Maywood Tile Co. in New Jersey. The factory had been making heating stoves and bought tiles from outside for decorating them. When they decided to make their own tiles they hired Wilde to superintend the operation. As he said, 'in those days, formulas and recipes were the private property of the ceramist; they were in fact, his capital.'[32] And so it was that the experts like Wilde sold their knowledge where they could; by 1900 Wilde was employed by the Providential Tile Co. at Trenton. Only a few months later, he joined the Robertson Art Tile Co. at Morrisville, Pennsylvania. It was not long before that pottery 'had an entirely new line of bright and matt coloured glazes and one of the best white wall tiles on the market.'[33] But by the summer of 1903, Wilde was off on his travels again and ended up in California, working with the Western Art Tile Co., which, at that time, was the only tile factory west of Indianapolis. Like Wilde, perhaps, men from the eastern states were attracted by the climate and untapped markets and travelled west to spread the industry. But as most were business-men, not ceramists, their only concern was to cash in on the trade, as quickly as possible. Wilde's description of the industry in California in the first decade of the century explains the difficulties that attended some of the early attempts at tile production. The story started with Joseph Kirkham who, after a brief association with the Providential Tile Co. in Trenton, established a business under his own name in Barberton, Ohio. This lasted no more than a couple of years and it was probably fortunate that the factory was burnt down in 1895. Kirkham then went to Tropico in California and set up the Kirkham Tile & Pottery Co. Fred Wilde takes up the story:

Mr Kirkham was always a plausible talker with a great imagination and came to Tropico, then a sleepy village, nine miles from Los Angeles, in 1898, and induced some of the people there to contribute toward building a tile factory. He found one or two capitalists in Los Angeles to provide cash. A Mr Richardson gave ten acres as a site. A Mr Chanler, a retired builder from Chicago, erected the brick buildings. One rancher contributed £20,000. Mr Kirkham never could make tiles commercially and of course failed. . . . After this failure, the factory was started again by L. Lindsay, a rich miner and E. M. Durant, a fine businessman, who bought the Tropico plant from the sheriff for 'a song' and paid the other creditors ten cents in the dollar. [Various men from Ohio and Trenton were engaged, but failed to do any good because they were specialists in electrical porcelains, not tiles; extraordinarily, the owners rehired Kirkham and he failed yet again.] . . . Some time after this, I [Wilde] came with the company . . . Unfortunately, these men from Ohio and Trenton had a body made for insulators, stilts, etc. [a clay mix unsuitable for tiles] and needed cone 10 or 11 [a high temperature] to vitrify their ware, and as the only clay they had for saggars was a low grade fireclay, the saggar cost was ruinous. Twenty-five per cent of the kiln space was taken up by empty saggars.

I had to rebuild the inside of the factory by degrees. They had a forty-leaf wooden [filter] press and two tanks for the slip below the floor; all the beaters were broken off, as they had been stopped by the high feldspar content in the body, and slip had run so thin that the body had settled solid in the tanks, and the pipes were nearly closed.

This meant plenty of worry and hard work until I got matters straightened out. Neither of the men had any knowledge of the business and came out every day grumbling and fault-finding because I could not produce goods . . . . We had to send to New York for all needs. Freight alone, on china clay and feldspar, was $30 per ton. This was certainly tough for the pioneers. I had been in Tropico several months before filling our first order. I saw our engineer writing on the wall and found out afterwards that he was marking the date of the first order shipped and produced from this factory during the five years it had been running . . . shortly afterwards I quit in disgust.[34]

This case illustrates the extraordinary difficulties of being a pioneer in an industry quite new to this part of America. But in the eastern states an efficient and more productive industry was growing up; not without difficulties, but not without successes.

One of the most accomplished manufacturers was the American Encaustic Tiling Co. of Zanesville, Ohio. The firm was established by Benedict Fischer in 1875 and through modest and careful development it grew to be a large and successful enterprise. They made large numbers of glazed wall tiles and encaustic floor tiles. Their work was of considerable importance to the progress of the industry. Technically the decorative panels were not dissimilar to some of Osborne's work at Low's pottery, but the style was very different (plate 41). This was characteristic of American tiles: the firms employed designers and modellers whose work gave a particular style to the products. The designs were less susceptible to direct imitation than the English transfer patterns and generally speaking the Americans were much more individualistic in their approach. Just as Osborne's work is immediately recognizable, so Herman Mueller's panels for the American Encaustic Tiling Co. have a particular style and manner. Some large pieces (12×18 in.) were made, such as the female water-carriers which are relief figures in Grecian style. Other panels were made up of eight, ten or fifteen tiles with designs of classical female figures and chubby children; the settings might be a terraced garden, with potted plants and creepers; single portrait tiles were also made. Some curious commemorative tiles were issued in April 1892 celebrating the opening of a new factory by the company. A public holiday was declared in Zanesville and 15,000 of these tiles were distributed.

A number of important gentlemen were associated with the American Encaustic Tiling Co., among them Emil Kohler (who was one of the earliest presidents of the American Tile Manufactuerer's Association), Karl Langenbeck and Herman Mueller, who together founded the Mosaic Tile Co., also in Zanesville, and the brothers Paul and Leon V. Solon, whose father M. L. Solon worked for Minton's for many years. That Leon Solon should have come to America suggests that he found more outlet there for the individuality of his talents. As well as the hand-painted plaques, like those executed at Minton's, Solon did faience work and a series of cartoon images of animals. For his work with the American Encaustic Tiling Co. he was to be awarded the Gold Medal for Applied Arts by the American Institute of Architects. The company won medals, too, at the Paris Exhibition in 1900 and the Pan American Exposition in 1901—by the turn of the century the American industry was well established and quite capable of competing with the Europeans and surpassing them.

The Rookwood Pottery is one of the most celebrated names in the history of American ceramics. The company was established in 1880 by Miss Maria Longworth Nichols (later Mrs Bellamy Storer) and owes its inception, at least in part, to the craze for decorating tiles. In the late seventies, there were many groups of amateur artists (the Women's Pottery Clubs); Miss Nichols simply extended the idea of decorating tiles to include marketing the products. It was a success and 'for the first time in this country, it was demonstrated that a non-commercial art product could command the appreciation of the American public.'[35] The Rookwood Pottery made a variety of tiles: faience plaques with relief decoration, and panels with animal designs or fruit and flowers (plate 40). Among the many artists at Rookwood were Ferdinand Mersman (modeller), Clara Chipman Newton, E. P. Cranch and Matt A. Daly. Cranch designed an amusing series of tiles to illustrate old rhymes and stories such as *Isaac Abbott* and *Giles Scroggins' Ghost*. Cranch was a well known Cincinnatti lawyer who had associations with Rookwood from the first. The old tales and humorous sketches of rural life in eighteenth-century New England, that he had collected himself, were published (1886) as a booklet by Robert Clarke & Co. of Cincinnati; the tile designs were used as illustrations. Cranch died in 1892, aged eighty-three.

For ten years (1877–87), a group of New York artists would meet regularly on Wednesday evenings to decorate tiles. Unlike Rookwood there was never any commercial interest, but with all the ladies' groups that were being set up, they thought, 'why not take up the tile decorating craze more deeply?' And so 'The Tile Club' was formed. At first a limited membership was planned, but the original twelve soon grew to nearly thirty. They met at members' studios and spent some of the evening painting pictures on eight-inch white tiles. Among the many members the best known were Edwin A. Abbey, Winslow Homer and Stanford White, illustrator, painter and architect respectively. *The Book of the Tile Club* was published in Boston in 1886. It was written by one of the members and tells the story of some of their meetings and the escapades of the Owl, the Beaver, the Saint, Chestnut and all their friends (each member had a nickname)—the club seems to have been like a more light-hearted version of the Pre-Raphaelite Brotherhood or one of the 'guilds' that were formed in England at this time. The Tile Club was not a significant force in the development of the industry but it does indicate the interest and enthusiasm that was generated by the subject in America.

A large proportion of the manufacturers made floor tiles. As in England this was often the staple trade for many companies, to which art tiles were a profitable side-line. Encaustic tiles were mostly imported and the American manufacturers concentrated on plain quarries and geometric tiles of all shapes and sizes up to six inches square. Interesting variations on the standard product were made by the United States Encaustic Tile Works. An amusing story is told about one set of tiles that was made in the nineties, for a smart saloon in Fort Worth which in those days was still a western outpost for cattlemen and cowboys. The tiles were about two or three inches square and had a recess in the centre to hold a coin; silver dollars and $10 or $20 gold pieces were cemented in and fitted flush with the face of the tile—altogether several hundred dollars were inlaid into the floor, surely one of the most unusual (and expensive) tile pavements ever made:

> The place was soon a mecca for cowboys and cattlemen, and of course the townspeople, as every one wanted to get the thrill of walking on $10 and $20 gold pieces. One morning a couple of men, who seemed to be workmen, came into the place with picks and shovels and told the bartender that the proprietor had sent them to take up the floor and install a new floor. They dug up the entire floor and hauled it away in a large wagon drawn by a couple of mules. When the

proprietor arrived at noon, his pet floor with all the gold and silver coins was gone. He immediately ordered more tiles of the same kind, and again adorned the saloon with a floor 'where you could walk on money.'[36]

The United States Encaustic Tile Works made many other more conventional tiles, using local marls from Indiana and clays for a white body from South Carolina and Kentucky. Natural gas was used to fire the kilns. Ruth Winterbotham was one of the chief modellers making glazed panels with embossed designs such as 'Dawn,' 'Midday' and 'Twilight'. Some of her work was on display in the Women's Building at the Chicago Fair (1893)—there were panels with female figures representing the 'March Zephyrs' and a less sentimental circular plaque, fifteen inches in diameter, with a frontier scene illustrating a wood-cutter at work, with bison, mountains and the setting sun in the distance. The company was probably founded in 1877 by William Harrison, cousin to President Benjamin Harrison, although there is conflicting evidence.[37] The receiver was called when Harrison's bank, which was affiliated with the tile business, failed in 1886. In the same year a new company was formed by Cooper, Picken and Landers. It is interesting that the Englishman Robert Minton Taylor had connections with the former business, early in the eighties.

Although information is often rather sparse, many other American manufacturers warrant attention. The history of the Trent Tile Co., for instance, has been very poorly documented, although it was one of the outstanding firms in America in 1910, employing some three hundred workers. William Gallimore and Isaac Broome were both employed there and they were famous modellers, but it is not known when they left or what work they did. Gallimore, who, according to Barber, was an experienced and well travelled man with a vigorous and characteristic style (his portrayal of boys and cupids was particularly pleasing), probably went to join the American Encaustic Tiling Co. in Zanesville. Broome was certainly later engaged by the Providential Tile Co. in Trenton. Here he established a considerable reputation with his large relief panels of hunting scenes, stags' heads, sportsmen and dogs. Broome was an interesting and versatile artist with a career that was typical of many American tile designers. He first became interested in ceramics at the end of the Civil War, when he went to Europe and visited many of the major museums. On his return, he set up a terracotta business in Pittsburgh and made vases, fountains and architectural faience. The public response was not good, however, and the project had to be abandoned. After this he turned to portrait painting for a few years before attempting to set up another company in 1871 (still an early date for the American ceramics industry). This time he was foiled by the Brooklyn City Board of Health and in disgust he gave up the attempt to establish his own business and subsequently worked for a number of different firms as chief modeller and designer. He was obviously respected in the trade since he was appointed with

General McLellan to report on the ceramics industry abroad, soon after the Centennial Exhibition.

After Broome left Providential, in 1890, he joined Beaver Falls Art Tile Co., a firm specializing in stove tiles with embossed portraits and heads, using transparent glazes in pale blue and purple-green greys. Broome extended the range of their products and executed several 'highly admired pieces' in a classical style, such as a six-inch tile of 'Sappho' (a female figure leaning on a harp), larger panels illustrating Poetry, Music and Painting, and some twelve-inch portraits, including one of Washington. He also specialized in mural decorations for libraries, dining-rooms and bathrooms. Broome's successor at Providential was Scott Callowhill, an Englishman whose two sons, Hubert and Ronald, were also employed as decorators. Callowhill had worked at Doulton's and the Royal Worcester Works in England and was able to introduce some new ideas to the company. The precedent for their gilt tiles is easily traced to Worcester and, with a variety of embossed designs as well, the firm met with early success in the field of decorated work. Callowhill also modelled some large relief panels which were refreshingly unsentimental.

Another important manufacturer was the Cambridge Art Tile Works which was a development of the Cambridge Tile Manufacturing Co. of Covington, Kentucky. The business was operated by the Busse brothers who employed a German tile maker, Heinrich Binz, when they started to produce glazed bricks. Within a few years (1887), they began to specialize in ceramic tiles and the name of the business was changed. They made stove tiles and brightly glazed ceramic decorations for architectural work, also some circular teapot stands. Ferdinand Mersman (who came from Rookwood) was the principal designer and Clem Barnhorn one of the modellers. Mersman studied at the Academy of Fine Arts in Munich and his tiles were more sophisticated than many of his contemporaries'—figurative designs like 'Winter' and 'Daughters of the Sea' were attractive pieces. The company concentrated on matching their domestic tiles to the rest of the scheme of interior decoration; their gold and ivory colours, which were very popular at the end of the century, were designed to harmonize with the fashion for light-coloured furnishing fabrics.

The American manufacturers were certainly active in the late-nineteenth century, producing tiles of a high standard and substantially different to those made in England. Barber remarked that 'it is to the broad extension of the Arts and Crafts Movement that we should look for the best results in artistic development in this country' and one particular characteristic of American tiles is the extensive production of hand-modelled designs, rather than the transfer-printed designs that were so popular in Britain. English tiles were still imported in large quantities and the Tariff Laws of 1890 were designed to protect the market for American manufacturers (a duty of up to fifty per cent *ad valorem* was payable on certain tiles in 1897). Tiles were not popular in the United States before 1880, and imports amounted to no more than a few thousand dollars annually.[38] But there was a steady increase after that date and in the five years before the First World War the figure was averaging $100,000. It should be remembered, however, that this was offset by domestic production valued at some five million dollars a year—clearly the major part of the market was supplied by American firms.

7 Morris, De Morgan and the Craft Tradition

Morris is credited as the leader of that handful of men who were responsible for the reformation of mid-Victorian art and design. It was central to his principles that the machine should be excluded from the production of 'true art' and this, necessarily, led to his rejection of the work of the Potteries. It has been suggested that the machinery and production techniques that were employed by the tile makers were the natural outcome of developments in the industry: a result of increased demand and efficiency. In relation to the commercial potters, there are two aspects of Morris's work that are of particular importance: first the ethics of the craft tradition, as De Morgan was to manifest them, and secondly, the changing tastes of the public for which Morris & Co. were, to some extent, responsible. It is difficult to separate cause and effect within a generation that witnessed such wide changes in outlook as took place at this time. Morris was not the first, nor the only man, to call for a reformation in the applied arts, but he is generally regarded as the central figure in the period.

Morris regarded the decorative element in design as a personal expression of the truth; there had to be integrity in the work. In this he followed Ruskin's teaching, rejecting the machine and re-establishing the traditions of the medieval craftsmen. For the 1862 Exhibition at South Kensington, the firm of Morris & Co. made stained-glass which was so perfect an imitation of the medieval examples that many people thought they had used genuinely old glass. Morris slowly evolved the ethics of design that he was later to express in his lectures and writings. But his opinions bore so little relationship to the contemporary situation that it is difficult to see how they could be immediately followed. Although he was to declare that 'I do not want art for a few, any more than education for a few, or freedom for a few', by denying the machine, he was to deny the possibility of extending his work beyond the limited and exclusive market which could afford it. In the 1880s, Morris to some extent reconciled himself to mechanical production; the proviso being that the machine should always be a servant—a tool that might successfully be employed by the artist. In the last two decades of the century, industrial manufacturers responded once the embargo against them had been lifted. Lewis Day, Voysey and Walter Crane worked as designers in the tradition of William Morris and were also involved with commercial production. It is to these men that we should look for real evidence of the Arts and Crafts Movement in the history of Victorian tiles.

Morris first became involved with tiles early in 1862, when he wanted to use them in a fireplace surround for the Red House. Naturally he

wished to paint them himself and so he set off to buy some suitable biscuit. With disgust, he discovered that no hand-made tiles could be
obtained in England at this time (in fact, this was untrue) and, rather
than go to Minton's, Copeland's or Maw's, he preferred to import plain
white tiles from Holland. Experiments ensued, using the small stained-
glass kiln for firing purposes. From this time on, tile decorating became
one of the many activities of the firm and a set of tiles with pictures
of Adam and Eve were to have been on show at the 1862 Exhibition,
although they were not displayed owing to a misunderstanding. In
the early years of the firm (Morris, Marshall, Faulkner & Co., later Morris
& Co.) Burne-Jones and Charles Faulkner's sisters, Kate and Lucy,
did most of the work.

Among the first designs was a panel illustrating the story of *Beauty
and the Beast* which was used as an overmantel in Birket Foster's house
in Surrey. It was designed by Burne-Jones in 1862—a set of six scenes
showing 'how a Prince who by enchantment was under the form of a
beast became a man again by the love of a certain maiden'. The images
are graphic and lively, but the colours are rather washy, predominantly
greens and browns. Another Burne-Jones design depicted the story of
Cinderella. On these tiles the colours were not properly developed and
the result is muddy. Clearly the firm never achieved the technical proficiency that might have been expected, knowing Morris's thoroughness
in other matters. There is little evidence of detailed research and
development of glazing techniques. Some of the tiles, however, do have
a rare beauty, with a delicacy in form and colour that is quite exceptional (plate 64). The tile painting was soon given into the hands of
Kate and Lucy Faulkner, while the men concentrated on more important
work. Designs were contributed by most members of the firm and their
friends: Rossetti and Madox Brown together produced a set of tiles,
illustrating the different occupations associated with the seasons and
the months of the year; they were used at Queen's College Cambridge
in 1873. Philip Webb drew a series of birds which were painted in pale
blues. Morris designed some of the conventional floral and diaper
patterns that were used to surround the figurative subjects—the 'Swan'
was a popular motif, others were called 'Daisy' and 'Rose'. But Morris
was never deeply involved in tile production and the sum total of the
firm's output was very small.

Morris & Co. were not successful with everything they attempted to
do. Although a wealth of talent was employed the results were enor-
mously varied. The products of the Craft Movement have been viewed
with a deference and respect that has excluded consideration of other
work. The professional potters, whether or not they used machines,
were clearly much better at making tiles and more proficient in the technical aspects of decoration and glazing. The work of Morris & Co.
is more closely related to that of the art tile decorators and the growth
of this section of the industry owes much to the firm. But companies
like W. B. Simpson's were never so particular about the biscuit they used
and quite happily bought from Minton's and Maw's; so it was not as

craftsmen that they learned their lessons but as painters. In fact, even De Morgan used dust-pressed tiles at various stages in his career, although he was not particularly happy to do so and preferred to buy from Poole rather than Stoke. He and Morris had a strong dislike for the North Staffordshire Potteries and De Morgan laughingly remarked on one occasion that he hoped that his pots murmured songs of 'Persia rather than Staffordshire . . . anything but Staffordshire'.

Morris died in 1896 and in the following year, Aymer Vallance published a review of his work. Full of extravagant praise, he said that 'the Ceramic Art, or rather that branch of it represented by the ornamentation of tiles, is another industry which owes its rescue from degradation to William Morris.'[39] This is untrue. The tile makers learned from Morris, just as everybody learned from Morris, but what they learned was not, perhaps, what Morris would have wished. Nobody in Staffordshire threw out his dust-press or took a sledge-hammer to his printing machine. There was a strong demand for decorated tiles from the popular market which craft processes could never hope to satisfy. Morris's contribution was in the general reform of decorative art. The novelty and freshness of his designs led to fashions that were to some extent taken up by the tile manufacturers. The small wooden panels, painted by Morris and Burne-Jones, that are to be found on the backs of chairs and on the doors of sideboards, have a direct connection with the use of tiles in furniture (plate 17). The floral designs for wallpapers and tapestries are matched by the host of tiles decorated with poppies, lilies and roses. The rather clumsy patterns of the early years, were superseded by figurative designs: flowers, birds — all the trappings of the Art Movement. Morris had said that if the machine had to be used, make the design 'mechanical with a vengeance'. That, unfortunately, would have emphasized the distinction between those who could afford 'art' and those who could only manage the machine; the manufacturers bowed to fashion and mass-produced what everybody wanted —art tiles.

Morris was never able to reconcile his own involvement in the Craft Tradition with his active socialism. For him there was a partial solution in the utopian vision of *A Factory as it might be*. Nothing less than the destruction of the capitalist system would fulfil his dream of work in art and art in life. So long as art was ruled by commercialism, what hope could there be for men to aspire to that truth and beauty which Morris believed was innate to humanity? But he was too intelligent not to realize the limitations of the concept. C. R. Ashbee, one of the leaders of the Arts and Crafts Movement, recalled hearing Morris speak:

Old Morris was delightful, firing up with the warmth of his subject . . . At length, banging his hand on the table: 'No!' said he. 'The thing is this; if we had our Revolution tomorrow, what would we socialists do the day after?' 'Yes—what?' we all cried. And that he could not answer. 'We should all be hanged, because we are promising the people more than we can ever give them.'[40]

Morris was first a poet, then a socialist and thirdly a designer. Chintz wallpapers, still less tiles, were never so important to him as poetry and ideas. His greatest contribution to the age was in ideas.

William De Morgan shared Morris's belief in craft and manual work, but was not so averse to employing ingenious mechanical devices where they could be of assistance. The two men, who were close friends, first met in the late fifties when Morris was sharing lodgings with Burne-Jones in Red Lion Square. Encouraged by Morris, De Morgan turned from painting (he had studied at the Royal Academy Schools) and for several years worked on stained-glass and furniture decoration. It was not until 1869 that he really turned his attention to tiles and began experiments in the basement of his house in Fitzroy Square. In many ways he was one of the truest exponents of the idea of craft industry, outside Morris's immediate circle. Working independently, he was able to develop his own ideas in design and decoration. And in his determination to learn the art of ceramics from the very beginning, his work exemplifies one of the fundamental principles of the Craft Movement.

De Morgan continued with his stained-glass until he left Fitzroy Square in 1872 and during these years he did his homework in ceramics. It was on glass that he first noticed that a trace of silver in the paint that he was using gave an iridescent sheen when it was fired. This led him to experiment with lustres on pottery. Lustre ware was popular earlier in the nineteenth century and had De Morgan gone to Staffordshire he could have learned in five minutes how it was done. But it was typical of his work and of one aspect of the period that the magic lay in rediscovery. That life and vitality were missing from so many of the mass-produced art products of the time was due, in part, to the lack of enthusiasm with which they were made. If the process was mundane, so was the decoration. In combination with his talents as an artist, De Morgan's insatiable appetite for research and discovery in technical fields enabled him to produce tiles that were unique, not just in design, but in some of the colours and decorative effects that he obtained. The results show both the strength and weakness of the craft potter: occasionally one sees evidence of the most elementary mistakes (notably in the firing)—mistakes which an industrial manufacturer could have corrected at once; at the same time there are subtleties in some of the tiles that could never be imitated. De Morgan's lack of commercial interest left him free from the pressures of efficiency and, more especially, mass-production.

After he burned the roof off the house in Fitzroy Square, De Morgan moved to Cheyne Row, Chelsea. The accident was the result of his attempt to fire kilns connected to an ordinary household chimney and, not surprisingly, the landlord asked him to leave. But in Chelsea he had an opportunity to build a proper kiln and set about the business of pottery in earnest. He employed assistants and soon opened a showroom. At first he continued to use tiles made by other potters (The Architectural Pottery, Carter's, Craven Dunnill, Wedgwood's and also some Dutch tiles) but as soon as the business became established, he started to make his own biscuit. De Morgan made his tiles from plastic clay ostensibly because he was convinced of their greater resistance to wet and frost. But then, of course, part of the ethos of being a craftsman was to make everything by hand.

For the same reason, De Morgan devised his own method for executing a repeating pattern. A transfer print, such as Copeland's used, would have been unthinkable. Instead, the outline of the design was pasted on to a sheet of glass and a copy drawn on tissue-paper from the other side. This image was filled in by the artist with chosen pigments, using a master drawing as a guide. In this way, each tile was completely individual, with slight variations in the outline and intensity of the colours. The tile itself, after a biscuit firing, was prepared with a coating of white slip, technically called an 'engobe', which had a dual purpose. De Morgan used a tile body with a high 'grog' content—that is a clay mix with a large proportion of coarse material which gave greater strength to the tile; this was brown in colour and the engobe gave a smooth white surface for the decoration; it also gave far greater brilliancy to the colours. The next stage was to combine the two elements: the tissue with the coloured pattern and the biscuit which had been specially prepared. The tissue was fixed to the tile with a light adhesive and powdered glaze sprinkled on top. In the heat of the kiln, the paper was burnt to ash, which floated away with the smoke.

There was certainly an ingenious simplicity in the method. It is typical of De Morgan to have devised a technique that not only solved problems (reproducing the design) but also had particular benefits. The use of an engobe was not a new idea: it was a standard way of covering a coloured earthenware body to give it a white surface. But the industrial potters, using a dust-pressed tile (with a low grog content), preferred to aim for whiteness in the body rather than over it. Their prime consideration was economy in time and effort—commercial considerations that never concerned De Morgan. His business was always shaky. Hand-made tiles were bound to be expensive—each tile was cut from plastic clay and dried separately between sheets of glass, every design was painted by hand—the expense was so great and the production so small that it was bound to be a disaster, economically. When, for health reasons, De Morgan had to spend half the year away from the pottery, living in Florence, his financial situation became particularly acute. But De Morgan's aim was to be an artist and to produce the finest tiles possible—money was irrelevant.

During the Chelsea period, De Morgan executed some 300 different designs. They show the development of a very varied range of flowers, birds, fishes, sailing ships and mythical beasts. Some of them are red lustre, others in a plain green glaze and after about 1875 he introduced the famous Persian tiles, which used deep purples, blues and greens, in imitation of the 'Isnik' designs of the fifteenth and sixteenth centuries. An important commission was carried out for Lord Leighton in about 1877, when De Morgan repaired and completed a set of Islamic tiles for the Arab Hall in Leighton House, Holland Park Road, London. It is a mark of his success that is difficult to distinguish the original tiles and those made by De Morgan. The first big contract during the Chelsea period came from the firm of Barnard, Bishop & Barnard who were 'art metal workers' from Norwich. Several thousand tiles, in a pattern that came to be known as 'BBB' (because the Norwich firm was first to use it), were sold during the thirty odd years that it was in production; it was one of the most popular designs that De Morgan made. The 'BBB' design was a stylized floral motif, best described as a sunflower—it certainly came about partly in response to the sunflower craze of the Art Movement, as well as having obvious associations with Morris patterns. It was made in many different colours and was one of a range of designs that used sunflowers, roses and carnations (plates 60 to 62).

During the six years spent with Morris at Merton Abbey (1882–8), the production of tiles continued but there were fewer new designs. De Morgan turned his attention to pots. In 1888 he moved to Fulham and went into partnership with Halsey Ricardo, an architect who shared his enthusiasm for ceramic tiles. The factory was to continue in Fulham until it closed in 1907, although the partnership with Ricardo was amicably dissolved in 1898. Many of the old designs were still in production, but the most interesting works of the period were the murals and tile panels. In the late seventies, when he was still at Chelsea, De Morgan had made some tile pictures for the Tsar of Russia's yacht, *Livadia*, which was built in Glasgow. A number of panels were also designed at Merton, but it was not until 1894, two years after he first went to Florence, that De Morgan received his largest single commission, to supply tiles for six of the P & O liners.

In Italy De Morgan employed painters to work for him and was able to send Ricardo not just new designs, but some completed colour sheets that could be put straight on to the biscuit and fired. The utility of his decoration process was proved again, though in an unexpected way. But without De Morgan's personal supervision, the factory lacked proper directive and the painters let the routine of work spoil the product. Ricardo's architectural practice prevented him from finding time to sort out all the problems, neither did he have the technical knowledge to do so. There were difficulties with the kilns and salt deposits kept appearing on the tiles. Fears of tuberculosis kept De Morgan in Florence all winter and it was not easy to run a factory by post. Reginald Blunt took over from Ricardo but there was little work during the last years and the factory was kept going mainly for the sake of the staff. The best of the stock was used, in 1906, for a house that Ricardo was building near Holland Park in London.

The affairs of the company were wound up the following year and until his death in 1917 De Morgan found more profitable work as a novelist. The pottery had relied so heavily upon the presence of one man and his particular genius, that without him it could not continue. De Morgan's only known appearance on the public platform was a paper that he delivered to the Society of Arts in 1892, on the history of lustre. *The Studio* wrote a complimentary review of his work but, at the turn of the century, when 'not to be new is to be nothing', De Morgan's thirty-year-old designs seemed rather outdated. He regretted the growing sterility of the standard patterns but he was not in a financial position to start afresh (his powers of invention were not at an end as the last designs demonstrated). He looked back with nostalgia to the happy days of research and experiment. (It was ironic that his writing was to bring in no mean fortune, but by then it was too late.)

As a manufacturer, De Morgan was an anomaly in the general perspective of nineteenth-century tile production. In the nineties, several firms followed his lead and started to produce lustre tiles. Maw's made some 'Persian Ware' which successfully copied the original Isnik patterns. But De Morgan's designs were so individual and his manufacturing process so esoteric, that his tiles had little in common with those of the contemporary industrial manufacturers. There were a few individual artists in the nineteenth century whose work bears the same stamp of artist-craftsman—Hannah Barlow's sgraffito panels, for instance. There is evidence that other tile makers had equally good glazes: Maw's obtained their 'transparent celeste' some years before De Morgan started decorating tiles. But nowhere else in the industry were so many talents brought together in the genius of one man.

8 Mural painting

The bulk of Victorian tiles were made for the domestic market. The decorative inserts into furniture, the hearth tiles and the fireplace surrounds, the small panels in the porches of suburban houses—they were all from the catalogue ranges of the different manufacturers. But there were a number of firms whose artistic expertise led them into the specialized market of hand-painted murals. In many ways this subject represents the crowning achievement of nineteenth-century tile production.

Ceramic murals and pictorial tile panels were painted with great skill and delicacy by the Dutch artists, and magnificent work from sixteenth-century Turkey and Persia may also be seen in many museums. The panels of the late nineteenth century represent some of the finest work of the period, carried out by firms like Simpson's, Carter's and Doulton's. An artist such as W. J. Neatby (1860–1910), who hitherto has received very little recognition, painted designs with such imagination and vigour that his work happily stands alongside the more illustrious artists of his time.

It was not until the 1867 exhibition, in Paris, that the English tile manufacturers thought of reviving ceramic painting and even then they needed the French (Sèvres) to show them the way. W. B. Simpson and Sons were the first to recognize the possibilities of the medium and in 1869 they added art tile painting to their accomplishments as house decorators. *The Builder* remarked, 'we quite agree with Messrs Simpson in believing that ceramic painting will hold an important place in decoration hereafter; the current is setting that way. . . .'[41]

Many of the early paintings on tiles were for panels to be placed over fireplaces. Simpson's exhibited an elaborate 'art tile chimney-piece' at the 1871 exhibition. Five years later at Philadelphia part of Minton's display was a similar *tour de force*: 'One of the main attractions,' says Jewitt, 'was a lovely chimney-piece composed of tiles richly painted with humming birds etc. and over it an exquisite painting of a mother and her child, executed with the most perfect artistic taste and feeling, on thirty tiles.'[42]

The earliest work of any consequence was done for the South Kensington Museum, in London. The Refreshment Rooms, opened in 1868, were covered from floor to ceiling with ceramic tiles (plate 102). The large panels in the Grill Room were designed in 1869–70 by Sir Edward Poynter (1836–1919). They illustrate a subject that was to become popular, almost perennial: the seasons and months of the year. The total effect is overbearing but the individual designs are attractive, with some fine pictures of young ladies battling against the elements, determined to keep a firm hold on their enormous cloaks (plate 99). The panels are set into a wooden framework that lines the walls; below them is a dado of ten-inch tiles with innumerable different scenes, all in blue. The tiles for the large panels were made by Robert Minton Taylor at Fenton and decorated at Minton's Art Pottery Studio, Kensington Gore, London, possibly by students from the art college. The link between the Fenton pottery and Minton's studio is interesting since it was in 1871 that Hollins brought the court case against Taylor for abusing his rights to the name of Minton (see Appendix). Clearly Taylor and Campbell (from Minton's) were working together on this scheme and it was not long afterwards that they joined forces to set up the Campbell Brick and Tile Co.

The ornaments for the new museum (now the Victoria and Albert Museum) were extraordinarily elaborate and although these were the only murals, there were tiles of one sort or another in almost every part of the building. It seems that every firm was given an opportunity to do some work and there were encaustic, geometric or mosaic pavements by all the leading companies. This was to be a showcase for national art and industry and no expense was spared. However, much of it was not to survive for long: the Ceramic Gallery (plate 101), which was covered with faience work, has been destroyed, although the panels in the Refreshment Rooms are still intact.

Another company involved in the work at South Kensington was W. B. Simpson and Sons. During the seventies the firm established a considerable reputation as decorators and tile painters. Their panels in Cardiff Castle (1876) were considered the most significant work to date. William Burges was the architect in charge of the restoration of the castle, which was owned by the Marquess of Bute. Tucked away at the top of Bute tower are twelve panels which surround a magnificent roof-garden, with peristyle, watercourt and fountains. The designs, by H. Walter Lonsdale, illustrate incidents in the life of the prophet Elijah, taken from the Book of Kings (plate 106). They are largely figurative, with little landscape detail; the bright tiles enhance the quality of the space which, with bare stone walls, might otherwise be gloomy and dark. The designs for the main panels were painted on to the biscuit and retouched overglaze. There is also a dado in rich, wine-coloured tiles, with crocodiles, elephants and lions painted in a thin *pâte sur pâte*.

Simpson's were strictly tile decorators and although a few of their tiles bear an embossed trade-mark on the back, they never actually made the biscuit themselves. Their mural work at Cardiff is unsigned but their monogram 'w.b.s. & s.' was usually displayed somewhere on the panels. Another set of murals executed by this firm (1874) can be seen in the West End of London, at the Criterion Theatre, Piccadilly Circus. As individual designs they are not striking, but the overall effect gives the foyer a unique period character. Opposite the theatre, on the stairway of a large store, there is another example of attractive tile work. Decorative tiles were used so extensively in the late-nineteenth century that it is possible to spot them in almost any town or city. So many tiles of every sort and description were used in shops, offices, public and private buildings, that it would be impossible to mention more than a few examples.

A set of tiles executed for a house in Glasgow, owned by Mr Macfarlane, were made by Copeland's in about 1875 and painted by R. J. Abraham, the son of the Art Director. A frieze, three feet high, was made for the billiard room and some more work was done for the bathrooms upstairs. The designs were intended as a narrative sequence showing the four sporting ages of a British gentleman. On one side were pictures of 'Health', with youths at play; next they grew to 'Strength' and manhood; on the third side, this early training on the playing fields was shown to lead to 'Courage' and heroic deeds were depicted, possibly in a colonial setting; and finally, there was 'Fortitude', with the endurance of the older man. Fortitude gave the strength, health and courage to lift the glass of port and continue the game of billiards. This habit of personifying the abstract and the abstruse was peculiar to the Victorians and there were many designs depicting Art and Beauty, Science and Nature (plate 98).

Some designers showed a more subtle approach: Carter & Co. produced an interesting range of ceramic murals for the Cambrian Distillery of London. *The Building News*, in 1886, considered Carter's the foremost company involved in the revival of mural pictures. They did a series of hand-painted panels with scenes of local interest. In the reign of Charles II, a celebrated murder took place near Leicester Square and this was the subject of a panel for the Distillery's premises in Cranbourne Street. A similar design was done for the Rising Sun, a public house in Blackfriar's Road. Both buildings have been destroyed. Tiles were used extensively in Victorian bars and restaurants. The Dog and Duck in Frith Street, Soho, has a wall covered with a repeating pattern of dogs and ducks; panels of famous scientists decorate the walls of the Café Royal, Edinburgh; sunflowers adorn the porch of the Crown and Anchor in Longton, Staffordshire. The Hotel Cecil, opened in London (1896) and thought to be the largest hotel in the world, used Doulton tiles throughout the main reception rooms and in the dining-room, billiard and smoking rooms on the first floor. The building was demolished in 1930. Perhaps the most splendid existing example is the work of William De Morgan at the Tabard Inn, Bedford Park, Chiswick, where over 600 tiles were used in the wall decorations.

Some of the most sophisticated decorative panels were done by Doulton's of Lambeth. It is not certain exactly when this firm became involved in decorating tiles, but towards the end of the century they were responsible for some of the finest ceramic paintings ever produced in England. Doulton's chief claim to fame was really in the field of sanitary and industrial products. In the 1860s the company started a studio workshop which was run in association with the Lambeth School of Art and it was here that many of the well known Doulton artists served their apprenticeships. Although some Hannah Barlow designs date from the 1870s, it seems likely that Doulton's were not concerned with tiles for architectural decoration until the last decade of the century. It is known that W. J. Neatby took charge of the architectural department in 1890 and his earlier training at Burmantoft's might well have led him to promote the tile side of the business.

In 1904 Doulton's published a small illustrated book entitled *Pictures on Pottery*, which introduces itself as 'a note on some hospital wall decoration recently executed by Doulton & Co. Ltd, Lambeth'. The history of tile painting was traced back to 3300 BC to the tiles in the British Museum that were made for the Egyptian palaces, built by Rameses II and III at Tel-el-Yahûddîyeh. Della Robbia's work in Florence (fifteenth century) was given as a precedent for using tile murals in hospital decoration. Doulton's themselves did extensive schemes at University College and Saint Thomas's Hospitals, London, and in the Children's Hospital, Paddington Green. At Saint Thomas's, the two children's wards, Lilian and Seymour, had panels illustrating nursery-rhymes and well known stories such as *Jack and the Beanstalk*. The murals in Lilian Ward, dated 1896, have survived and are still in perfect condition. There were some doubts about using tiles in hospitals; they appeared to provide a highly functional and hygienic surface, but in 1900, the *Pottery Gazette* refers to the 'frequence of crazing observed in decorative panels and architectural pieces'. Even if the tile was flawless at the time of fixing, it was liable to craze since the biscuit absorbed a small amount of moisture and through expansion, the glaze might break. In the cracks, germs could breed. It is a tribute to Doulton's work that this has not happened.

In Lilian Ward the panels are surrounded by tiles with a dirty green glaze which hardly displays them to advantage. But the panels themselves are varied and exciting: Red Riding Hood (plate 114), Jack and Jill, Cinderella, Dick Whittington, Miss Muffet and Jack the Giant Killer. For three-quarters of a century, Little Boy Blue has been trying to get the sheep out of the corn and Sleeping Beauty has been waiting for the Prince to wake her up. Each picture depicts the essential moment of drama in the story and although the lines are clear and bold, there is sufficient detail to warrant quite close examination. Generally speaking, mural painting should be rather like a stained-glass window: immediate impact is most important as detailed drawing is lost. But these panels include a certain amount of naturalistic detail that would appeal to a child. The brambles that surround Sleeping Beauty's bed are drawn with the freedom and movement that is typical of the 1890s (plate 114). The falling tresses of her golden hair and the loose folds of her dress are evocative of many similar pictures that were illustrated in *The Studio*.

In 1888 Doulton's started making their 'Carrara Ware'. They had a special recipe for an opaque glaze that fired slightly gloss, similar in appearance to the brilliant white marbles from the Carrara district of Italy. The technique was used extensively in architectural work and was always a feature of Doulton's stand at the international exhibitions. Production of this faience formed a large part of the output of the firm's architectural department, to which mural painting was really an auxiliary. But in the ten years around the turn of the century, Doulton's did a large number of schemes that included decorative panels. For the Chicago Exhibition of 1893, eight panels were made, illustrating themes such as Agriculture and Commerce and the life of Columbus. These were designed by J. Eyre and painted by J. H. Mclennan. Two pictures which received special attention were done by the Lewis sisters: Miss Esther's 'Millstream', and 'Night Flowering Cactus' by Miss Florence. The sisters were thought to be very gifted artists by contemporary critics.

In the nineties, W. J. Neatby was in charge of the architectural department at Doulton's. He came from Yorkshire and had already worked for ten years at Burmantoft's in Leeds. He did not have the benefit of an art school education and his only artistic training was the few years that he spent working for an architect, as a boy. What he learned about ceramics he learned by experience. In a review of his work in *The Studio*, Aymer Vallance says that it is 'the strength of Mr Neatby's work, that he is no mere theorist, but at once a designer, vivid in imagination and a handcraftsman who has thoroughly mastered the ways and means of his material.'[43] In this, Neatby exemplified the traditions of the Arts and Crafts Movement and much of his time at Doulton's was spent investigating novel techniques for glazing and colouring ceramics. As an artist-craftsman he found plenty of scope for his talents in painting murals and did not seem bothered by the commercial constraints that a ceramics factory imposed upon his work. Indeed, he probably had greater freedom to work and experiment as he chose, in this situation, than he would have had if faced by the constant pressure of financial exigencies as was De Morgan. But by the turn of the century, he wanted to expand the range of his activities and until his death in 1910 he worked in partnership with E. H. Evans, making stained-glass, furniture and metalwork, essentially in the style of contemporaries like C. F. A. Voysey.

Neatby is known to have been directly responsible for many of Doulton's ceramic murals, but most of them have been destroyed. For the John Lines showroom, in Tottenham Court Road, London, he designed six panels which were 'studies in harmony and colour'; a set of medallions illustrating the history of costume were made for the Theatre Royal, in Birmingham. But these were modest schemes by comparison with the Freemasons' banqueting hall, described by P. G. Konody, writing for a German magazine in 1903:

On the first floor of Frascati's restaurant, once the meeting place of London's fashionable world, but long since superseded by more modern and luxurious places, there is a remarkably constructed irregular space, used as an assembly room and banqueting hall for several Freemason lodges, and reserved for this purpose. At one end, not in the middle, the ceiling bulges out in a cupola shape. The walls are divided by pilasters into fields of different sizes, which are surmounted by flat arches and terminate about six foot six inches above the floor in a wooden strip which surrounds the entire space. The empty surface of the cupola and walls are provided with ceramic paintings glowing with colour, allegories and symbols of Freemasonry. Four female figures on the cupola correspond to the four axes of the world. Their skin and hair reflect in their climatic distinctions the extent of Freemasonry over the inhabited earth. These figures stand on wavy lines which surround the rim of the cupola like branches and which, as in Egyptian hieroglyphics, represent the flux of existence. The white clothed figures are provided with shields on which are depicted the symbols of the chief lodges of the North, South, East and West. On the large arch-shaped walls (the fourth wall is furnished with windows which allow no space for such large areas) Freemasonry is represented as the tamer of human passions. These three decorative paintings, executed in flat tones, are almost geometrical in the conventional symmetry of their arrangement. The majestic figure of a woman is enthroned in Byzantine hierarchy in the middle. Three panels frame pairs of leopards, enormous snakes and peacocks, which are fettered to the chains which hang in regular curves from both her hands. Thus does the spirit, which is the principle of Freemasonry, bridle the passions and vices, symbolized by the three types of animal: brutal strength and power, low spite and cunning and vanity and pride. The space which is feebly daylit by two quite inadequate leaded windows, wears a peculiarly festive air at night, when the electric lamps, distributed over the ceiling, are lit. One can hardly think of a better assembly place for the Freemasons.[44]

Another attractive set of designs, painted by Neatby in 1896, was for the Winter Gardens in Blackpool (plate 108). Twenty-eight panels formed an arcade for the main entrance, with life-size pictures of girls in Pre-Raphaelite costumes. A mirror was set between two panels in each bay; two mirrors, on opposite sides, gave the impression of an 'arcade' at right-angles to the thoroughfare, with an infinite number of reflections. Neatby's treatment of the subject, although showing a keen appreciation for Art Nouveau and the work of the Pre-Raphaelite painters, reveals an independence in his style that gently mocks at both. The essence of the 'aesthetic' costume in the 1880s, was the long swirling draperies and the haphazard combination of clothes, preferably with some naturalistic ornament. This Neatby developed to the point of burlesque: with the aesthetic peacock feathers and Byzantine decoration, he makes reference to most of the ideas that were current at the time.

It seems likely that Neatby used his first wife, Emily, as a model for these paintings. She had the air of a Rossetti maiden with the delicate features and slender figure that he so much admired. It is said that he was so jealous of possible admirers that he kept her shut up at home with the blinds permanently drawn. But though Emily may have had good reason to look sad, Neatby's figures are full of life and vigour. There is nothing of that 'hang-dog' look that is characteristic of the work of Rossetti and Burne-Jones. Neatby's paintings are sensitive and graceful with neither the aesthetic melancholy, that W. S. Gilbert parodied in *Patience*, nor the morbid introspection of the Art Nouveau artists.

Neatby's most exciting murals were for the Meat Halls at Harrods in Knightsbridge (1902). The layout is little changed today, although the glass roof has been removed, as a result of additional building on the floors above. Again, Konody gives a lively description of the premises:

> At the centre of the labyrinth of departments, leading into and out of one another, is a glass roofed provision hall for the sale of meat and venison, a remarkable space whose layout in the lower part can best be compared with that of a triple-aisled church, whereas its super-structure resembles the barrel-vaulted roof of the famous palm house at Kew. The roof is supported on rectangular piers and is vaulted in several sections over the 'nave', while the goods are displayed on broad marble tables along the walls of the 'aisles'. The floor is laid out in a most pretty pattern of large white and small black marble [geometric] tiles and the walls, the vaulting beneath the glass cupola, the ceiling over the aisles, in short everything that is not glass or marble, is clad in glazed pottery tiles. The space is airy, high and clean, splendid in its colour matching and looks more like an exhibition than a market hall. The piers are white and striped into thin light yellow bands, similar to mosaic. The spandrels of the glass vault, which rest on them, start vertical and then turn inwards higher up. On the vertical surfaces, there are twenty circular glazed tile pictures of hunting and herding scenes . . . .
>
> In the smaller fields on the long walls are repeated, at regular inter-vals, a number of birds with splendidly coloured plumage, so that the decoration of the space forms a kind of idealized catalogue of the foodstuffs for sale there.
>
> The strongly emphasized quadrature of the tiles defines the nature of the material and the peculiar appropriateness of its method of treat-ment. The colour ranges in the wreaths of decoration from the deep blue-green tones of the water upwards into pure white, for the whole space is kept as light as possible. The light streaming in from above is reflected from the walls, the floor and the marble counter-tops, so that the shadows in the darkest corners are dissolved. Great care has been taken for the ventilation and coolness so that even on the hottest summer days, the space is comfortable to stay in, without the otherwise repellent smells of such places. Architecturally and decoratively alike, this provision hall is a triumph of original modern style and in the practical application of sound principles.[45]

The images are drawn in what can best be described as a rural English Art Nouveau style. They are simple and modest; broad areas of colour are defined by bold black lines used to give a constant rhythm to the decorations. Wherever possible, a line is turned into ornamental motif, but the composition does not have that sinuous delicacy that is associated with the work of Mackintosh and the Glasgow Four. Neatby relied more on the natural shape and movement of the animals and figures (plate 109). The effect is both decorative and dramatic, elements essential to ceramic murals.

There are many pointers here as to how ceramic tiles could be used to advantage in the applied arts of the nineteenth century. Tiles were the most suitable material to provide a decorative surface. The colours were permanent and bright, the surface was impervious and easy to clean and since the glaze could be highly reflective, the lighting was well distributed. As for the decoration itself, anything was possible. But strong clear images, with only the suggestion of detail, were more effective than a delicate painting with subtle gradations of tone and colour. Art with a capital 'A' was more suited to canvas than tiles. Another important factor was the character of the pictures: a Landseer painting of deer on the craggy braes would probably send every customer to the vegetarian juice counter. The designs had to be graphic, without being too lifelike and in this, too, Neatby was successful.

Doulton's work has been singled out for particular attention since they mastered the essential features of the medium so well. Albert Slater, working at Minton Hollins's, painted a number of tile pictures; four of them, until recently, decorated the walls of the swimming baths at Longton, built in 1886 (plates 103 and 107). But they lack the essential vigour and imagination of the 'Lambeth Faience' panels. Some other work can be seen at the Mayfair premises of Thos. Goode & Co. (plate 113). The paintings on the outside of the building (1876), with parrots, humming-birds and butterflies, are typical of the Japanese taste of the period. The panels may have been painted by W. B. Simpson & Sons and, although the tiles are rather weathered, they are still fine examples of mural painting. The designs were painted on brown biscuit, predominantly in white. With birds positioned dramatically on slender branches and a minimum of landscape detail, the painter has successfully imitated the elements of Japanese art.

Ceramic murals were made individually for particular clients, in contrast to the majority of decorative tiles for the popular market. It is significant that this was really the province of the art tile decorating companies. These enterprises were definitely commercial in outlook but could indulge their talent as artists only in the context of the industry as a whole. The smaller firms executed designs in a variety of media and relied on companies like Minton's for tiles and Wenger's for colours. They were working as a production industry, not as manufacturers. The decorating companies responded to the fashion for art tiles for a few decades but they could turn their attention elsewhere and concentrate on wallpapers, furniture and metalwork, as they chose. But the manufacturers had invested in tiles and all the plant and machinery needed to make them. The business was an industrial concern and not just the loose association of a few like-minded artists. And so, when the fashion changed, mural painting came to an end. But the mass-production of tiles continued. Perhaps more emphasis was laid on the use of tiles as a building material and less on their artistry and good taste. The industry also survived by joining in cut-price warfare (which signalled the demise of the first Tile Association in 1902*) and hand-painted work was priced out of the market.

* The Plain, Encaustic and Earthenware Tile Manufacturers Association was formed in 1889. It was chiefly concerned with establishing minimum prices for standard products; it also compiled a list of credit-worthy dealers who were eligible for discounts. But the influence of the organization was severely handicapped since its membership was incomplete. The Association was disbanded in 1902 but was re-formed a few years later.

9 Architectural faience and terracotta

In England, very few buildings used decorated tiles externally. Although Middle Eastern cities had traditionally employed ceramics in architecture, with shining minarets and lustred domes, the weather (supposedly) had always ensured that Victorian cities were a uniform drab grey. The use of colour had been largely neglected, just as it is today. As a result, P. G. Konody, continuing his review of Neatby's work, was pleasantly surprised by a building he had seen in Bristol.

Quite recently an especial building was executed in one of the main streets of Bristol, an industrial and mercantile town noted rather for its smoke, dirt and uncommonly heavy rainfall than its outstandingly splendid modern buildings. At first glance the façade looks like that of a richly painted temporary exhibition building. A closer inspection discloses that the peculiar effect of colour is not due to painting in the immediate sense of the word. A fresco painting would be quite out of place in such a climate. One need only think of the forty year old murals inside the Houses of Parliament—the climate is nowise nastier than Bristol—which were recently freed from their protective coating and to the general consternation, turned out to be hopelessly ruined; so upset by atmosphere and humidity, so darkened and cracked, that we can hardly recognize the subjects any more. Even mosaic has been shown to be useless for street decoration. The mosaic decorations exposed to the weather on the façade of St James's Hall, which are about to fall into the hands of the demolition firms, are nothing more today than unrecognizable black stripes.

The façade of the Bristol building [plate 110], which is Mr Edward Everard's printing works, consists from top to bottom of polychrome ceramics. The purely architectural decoration is confined to two decorative turrets with domes, supported on columns either side of the pyramidical termination above the top floor. The building itself is executed in blocks of matt-surfaced terracotta. Ornamental and figurative decoration such as the frieze over the ground floor, the angel in the spandrel between the two first floor windows, the image of Gutenburg, father of printing, and William Morris, the bold innovator who has made craft back into art and the allegorical figure of truth, with a mirror and lamp, are all made of glazed tiles. The effect of the colour is increased by the glowing enamelled areas of the entrance grill and other details.

It would be a laughable exaggeration to praise the façade of the Everard press as though it were a faultless work of art. But its shortcomings lie largely in the insuperable difficulties with which an unaccustomed material confronted the architectural treatment; and the advantages which this choice of material carries with it are so striking, that the building can be designated as a bold and almost epoch making experiment, as a first step in a direction full of promise for future development. It demonstrates the possibility of designing a more colourful and hospitable street image than the otherwise very dark, grey industrial towns of England and that, not temporarily, with means which cannot long withstand the influences of the weather, but lastingly. Rain, which in most English brick buildings merely drives the grime and soot deeper into the material has the opposite effect here and helps the façade keep its original cleanness and freshness. The fired colours are permanent and unfading, the smooth surface disdains the dirt and each downpour acts as a further detergent. And if the scheme of architectural composition and figurative ornament leaves much to be desired, the effect of the colours witnesses to a splendid artistic taste and makes the building distinctly remarkable among all the dark routine and rather depressing buildings which surround the Everard press.[46]

The Everard building was completed in 1902 and caused quite a stir locally when the drapes were pulled off this strange monument to the printers' craft. It is still something of a surprise to come across it today, tucked away in a small street in Bristol, surrounded by the pompous portals of neo-classical architecture.[47] It was the first and almost the last example of an attempt that was made to use polychrome ceramics for external decoration.

The idea had been contemplated in the early seventies when a correspondent in *The Builder* suggested that 'the capabilities and advantages of the material, being so great as to durability, cleanliness etc, and hence its suitability to the dirty and destructive atmosphere of large towns, could it not be employed upon a thorough system for the external facing of buildings?'[48] And the short answer was, 'no'. Basically it was a matter of technology: the tiles were not strong enough to withstand the damp, the surface would craze and the body crack in the frost. Worse still they would fall off when water got in behind and softened the fixing; the Underground Railways were painfully rich in examples of these failures. Nonetheless, the façade of a building called for as much attention as the interior decorations and since tiles were impractical at this time another answer had to be found and the natural material to use was terracotta.

Terracotta was impervious and because it was fired at a relatively low temperature the pieces could be quite massive. The large blocks were often set twelve or fifteen inches into the wall and became integrated with the whole structure of the building. Elaborate friezes and grotesques could be made and although the colour range was limited to buffs, browns and reds, some very decorative effects could be achieved. Terracotta was often cheaper than stonework and harder than the soft stone that was used for much of the ornamental carving on the neo-Gothic buildings (witness the deterioration of the decorative work on the Houses of Parliament). The standard pieces were made from moulds which ensured an accurate repetition of units and any particularly difficult panels of figurative work would be modelled by hand. This allowed for more detail and undercutting to throw the image into better relief. With terracotta the decoration was almost always three dimensional and following the Gothic revival there were a host of pinnacles, minarets and whatnots made for the town halls and hotels. The Russell Hotel (1898) is a typical example. In Kensington, the Victoria and Albert Museum used terracotta ornament quite extensively. This sort of architectural decoration coincided with the heyday of the encaustic tile and the two elements can often be seen together. As with decorative floor tiles a cheap imitation of the grandiose public buildings filtered through the architecture of middle-class suburbia. Property speculators budgeted for external decoration and one of the most popular forms of 'architectural enrichment' was small panels of terracotta on the walls. Variations on the sunflower theme were most common, although some of the mansion blocks had quite elaborate panels with the name of the building, its date and some suitable motif.

One of the most elaborate terracotta façades was made by Doulton's for Harrods, in 1902. By this time the material was rather *passé*, but it provided decoration that was striking and politely ostentatious, without the scandal of being *avant garde*, like the Bristol building, completed in the same year. By the turn of the century, ceramic tiles were becoming a quite acceptable material for facing a building. But before the experiment at Everard's, only plain glazes had been used, usually a drab yellow-brown (plate III). At first it looked as though the idea would catch on and the streets of London would be filled with rainbow colours. Certainly Halsey Ricardo and Walter Crane were doing their best to promote the idea. In a paper to the Society of Arts, entitled 'Art and Life in the Building and Decoration of Cities' (1896), Ricardo strongly advocates the use of coloured decoration in towns and on another occasion he explains why:

> The result of this stony scholarship of our streets is that we can't live in them. Every evening thousands escape by every railway from the masterpieces of correct architecture . . . to the shelter of the country where the earth is green about them and the heaven blue above them. Cannot we make our streets a little more kindly and comforting to those poor prisoners who cannot escape? We have tried mass and form and light and shade; might we not now have an attempt at colour?[49]

Polychrome ceramic tiles were the most suitable form of external decoration. In 1906 Ricardo built a house in Addison Road, Kensington, for Sir Ernest Debenham (who owned a store in Oxford Street) and as well as the extensive De Morgan work inside, much of the outside of the building was faced with ceramic tiles. The colour scheme was predominantly blue, green and white, with some fine panels in the covered entranceway. The De Morgan Pottery closed in 1907, otherwise more work of this sort might well have been done.

Already the mood of functionalism was creeping into architecture, however. The decorative element of tiles as external cladding for building became increasingly unimportant. They were a useful building material, but the potential offered for colour and design was never fully exploited. Glazed bricks provided a cheaper and more practical alternative and there were a number of schemes which devised geometrical ornament in black and white. The lack of enthusiasm which the English showed in this matter may well have had something to do with their distaste for the 'decadence' of the New Art on the Continent. Sir Nikolaus Pevsner describes the Everard building as the 'wildest Art Nouveau' and Art Nouveau certainly did not go down well with most of the English architects: there was only 'the promise for future development', which never came.

10 Developments in the industry

In 1800 North Staffordshire was a rural area, only a few potteries and scattered towns nestled in the green valleys. A hundred years later, as Arnold Bennett described it in his novels, it was a wilderness of pot and cinders. From a cottage industry where a master craftsman engaged a few apprentices, a factory system took over in which owners might employ several hundred workers. Soon the Six Towns fused into one large conurbation, 'pot banks' sprouted like mushrooms and the network of roads, railways and canals linked The Potteries to the world. The tile manufacturers were not simply potters but became involved in international trade, politics and local government. They were not profound thinkers nor social reformers, but businessmen in an industry that was typical of the age. The period was one of commerce and trade, with a growth of consumer markets and the development of mass-production techniques. No evidence will be found of fine ideals and romantic philosophies.

The inevitable results of the rapid expansion of industry, with its emphasis on financial success, were the appalling conditions in which men, women and children were employed. Lead poisoning and silicosis kept the level of life expectancy below the national average. Clay dust slowly filled their lungs and the fine particles of flint and stone ground their way into the tissues of the skin.

During the 1890s new laws were introduced to give greater protection to the factory workers. The Employers Liability Bill of 1893 caused the Tile Association members some anxiety and it was suggested that they should form 'a common fund out of which claims should be paid and vexatious actions defended'. The same question arose over the Workmen's Compensation Act in 1897 and in order to gauge the extent to which the industry was prone, eleven member firms listed the accidents that had occurred on their premises during the last year: six companies had no accidents at all, one man had a cut hand which had kept him away from work for eight weeks; Wooliscroft's had one fatal accident; Pilkington's, one pinched finger; Craven Dunnill's, one accident as a result of a boy throwing some tiles at another—he slipped and broke his leg; J. C. Edward's had had two accidents during the last three years.

It was considered to be quite a good record and unlikely to involve the management in any great expense. But the new regulations about overalls, head coverings, ventilation and medical examinations looked as though they might cause trouble. Nobody objected to improving conditions, provided that they did not have to bear the expense.

It was not until the end of the century that any government action was taken against lead poisoning. After much correspondence in the newspapers, the Home Secretary appointed Professors Oliver and Thorpe, in 1899, to prepare a report on the subject. At a Tile Association meeting, two years earlier, the manufacturers had suggested that a handwash of soda sulphate was an effective prevention. It was stated that the chief drawback was the neglect of the workmen themselves, since they did not bother to use the appliances provided (such as Wenger's patent respirators).

The only widespread strikes in the pottery industry had been in the 1830s when some employers made drastic reductions in wages in order to make their prices more competitive. Trade unions were organized and the owners responded by forming the Chambers of Commerce, in order to protect their own interests. On this occasion, the masters won the battle. But unions were to be legally established and they protected and assisted their members wherever possible. During the second half of the century, the trade unions took a responsibility for the general welfare of the workers that the Factory Acts were later to make the legal responsibility of the management. But the relationship between management and employees in the tile industry appears to have been relatively amicable and the picture was more one of benevolent patriarchs than capitalist tyrants. One firm (Craven Dunnill's) even went so far as to share among the men any profit in excess of a ten per cent dividend paid to shareholders.

During the nineteenth century, most pottery craftsmen were paid on piecework. The labour problems during the 1830s were partly the result of a move to make payment on the basis of 'good from the kiln' rather than 'good from the hand'. It is not known for certain how far this operated in the tile industry. But there are stories of a pottery master who would walk into the throwing shop, cane in hand, and smash any piece of work that was imperfect. This obviously hit at the pocket of the man who made the pot, not the profits of the owner. Craftsmen were traditionally employed on an annual contract, at a price that was negotiated each year. One of the early concerns of the trade unions was to standardize the wage structure. As for the owners, their profits were their own and in many cases their involvement in the daily running of the factory was marginal. When Hollins (known locally as 'the Colonel'), built his factory at Shelton, New Road it was so designed that he could drive round in his gig to inspect the premises. A gentleman potter might visit, but should not get his feet dirty.

Managers and foremen took much of the immediate responsibility. At Maw's, Mr B. Suart was in charge of the factory and even represented the company at Tile Association meetings (M. D. Hollins was the first President). The important business was usually handled by the owners, however, particularly the international exhibitions. Big firms like Minton's, Campbell's, Maw's and Malkin Edge were well represented abroad and James Malkin, for instance, made several world tours to promote foreign trade. At home these men were involved in public life: Colin Campbell was a particularly well known local dignitary; he was High Sheriff of the County, a Justice of the Peace, Mayor of Stoke for three successive years from 1880, and for six years (1874–80) Parliamentary member for North Staffordshire. In 1867, he became a director of the North Staffordshire Railway Co. and was later chairman of the board—he would have the train stopped when it passed his house, so that he could get off without the trouble of going to the station! Others of these wealthy gentlemen helped to build town halls, churches, hospitals and schools.

The heritage of the Victorian potters is still very evident in North Staffordshire, even though most of the old 'pot-banks' have been demolished. As a result of interest in industrial archaeology the Staffordshire Pottery Industry Preservation Trust has been formed to build a living museum for the pottery industry in and around Stoke-on-Trent. The museum is sited at the old Gladstone Pottery in Longton, which has not been substantially altered since it was built in the middle of the last century. The enclosed courtyard, with its towering 'bottle-ovens', contrasts vividly with modern tile factories where automatic presses and conveyors crowd the production floors.

The tile industry has changed as much in the last seventy years as it did during the nineteenth century. Tiles are still used in a great variety of ways, but modern methods of production employ sophisticated machinery, new materials and different techniques of decoration. Automatic screen-printing has replaced the old method of transfer printing; conveyors carry an uninterrupted procession of tiles under a waterfall of glaze, which ensures a perfect and even coating; an abstract pattern of colour is often sprayed on, automatically, as the conveyor carries the tile onwards to the tunnel kilns. Everything in the highly organized manufacturing plant is designed for speed and efficiency.

These changes have been made possible, not only by the developments of modern industrial technology, but by the gradual changes within the tile industry itself, which have taken place throughout this century. By 1900, most of the tile manufacturers had settled to a particular formula in the design and production of their work, and the Tile Association was able to fix minimum prices for standard products. A firm such as Minton's continued to produce some exclusive and highly specialized tiles with elaborate hand-painted patterns, but most of the manufacturers were simply working with transfer prints and embossed majolica ware. Art Nouveau and the changing styles of the new century brought fresh designs, but the techniques of decoration were to be substantially the same for many years to come. Large numbers of these simple majolica tiles can be found, with bright green, purple or blue glazes. A small line motif replaced the elaborate floral patterns of the Victorian tiles. After the First World War, plain or mottled glazes were used on the majority of tiles. And just as the range of products was rationalized, so the larger manufacturers grew and took over the many smaller tile concerns. Today there are only two major manufacturing companies in Britain.

The revival of Victorian decorative art must have some impact upon the production of modern ceramic tiles. In recent years, old processes such as tube-lining have been revived and modern murals have been made by the industrial tile manufacturers—once more the decorative qualities of the medium are being exploited. H. and R. Johnson has revived the traditional craft of making encaustic tiles and has done extensive restoration work in the Palace of Westminster, as well as in the Smithsonian Institute and Capitol Building in Washington. But while old-fashioned processes may be employed for a small amount of specialized work, modern techniques will continue to be used for mass-producing tiles. This calls in question the nature of modern decorative art. It would be fatuous to suggest that modern tile manufacturers should make their products in the same way as the Victorian potters. Although many contemporary tiles have sterile and unimaginative designs, there would be no point in returning to antiquated production processes in an attempt to achieve better .results. In many ways, this situation is paralleled by that of a century ago when Morris revived craft processes in order to combat a similar problem.

98 Pair of panels personifying Art and Nature by Maw & Co., *c.* 1880; such personifications were favourite themes for Victorian painters. These designs are predominantly dark blue with brown outlines and shading. Collection H. & R. Johnson-Richards.

99 Two of Poynter's original drawings for panels in the old Grill Room at the Victoria
& Albert Museum. By permission Victoria & Albert Museum, London.

100 Ceramic murals in the old Grill Room. The work was completed 1874. The panels
were designed 1869-70 by E. J. Poynter and painted at Minton's Art Pottery, Kensington Gore, on biscuit made by Robert Minton Taylor at Fenton. Victoria & Albert
Museum, London.

101 The old Ceramic Gallery at the Victoria & Albert Museum, now modernized.

102 The old Refreshment Rooms at the Victoria & Albert Museum. The tiles here, as in the Ceramic Gallery (plate 101), were majolica ware made by Minton, Hollins & Co., designed by J. Gamble. The work was completed in 1868. The inscription round the walls reads: 'There is nothing better for a man than that he should eat and drink and that he should make his soul good in his labour XYZ.' Victoria & Albert Museum.

103 Minton, Hollins & Co., painted by Albert Slater; 1886. One of four panels made for the swimming baths at Longton, Staffordshire. By permission City Museum, Stoke-on-Trent.

104 Maw & Co., *c.* 1875; the ubiquitous sunflower.

105 Grueby Faience Co., *c.* 1895; one of a series of woodland scenes, 13 in. Smithsonian Institution, Washington DC.

106 a

106 b

107 Tile mural by Minton, Hollins & Co., painted by Albert Slater 1886. Four panels with scenes of bathing, skating, ploughing and bringing home the hay were made for the swimming baths at Longton (see plate 103). By permission City Museum, Stoke-on-Trent

Opposite
106 Murals by W. B. Simpson & Sons, for the roof gardens in Bute Tower, Cardiff Castle (1876). The panels illustrate stories from the Book of Kings, with Hebrew inscriptions.

108 Doulton & Co., W. J. Neatby designs for the Blackpool Winter Gardens; 1896. The mirrors on either side of the arcade reflect the panels. By permission Blackpool Tower Co.

109 Doulton & Co., W. J. Neatby designs for Harrods' Meat Halls, forming an idealized catalogue of the goods for sale. By permission Harrods, Knightsbridge.

110 Doulton & Co., the Everard
Building, Broad Street,
Bristol; designed by W.
J. Neatby, 1901. One of
the very few attempts in
Britain to use polychrome
tiles externally. Country
Life.

111 Ceramic façade in Gloucester Road, London; c. 1890.
The tiles are predominantly
brown and yellow.

112 Tile panels in Japanese style at premises of Thos. Goode & Co., don. The manufacturer is not knc the building was completed 1876. permission Thos. Goode & Co.

113 Details of plate 112.

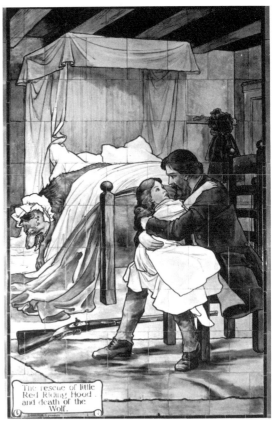

114 Tile murals in the Lilian Ward for children, St Thomas's Hospital, London. Courtesy of the Board of Governors, St Thomas's Hospital, London.

Suuflower

Warwick - I love no colours,
I pluck a White Rose
with Plantagenet.

HUMOUR. 1598

A Most perfect Toledo I assure you sir

Cap. Bobadil

You talk of Morgaly, Excalibur, Durindana or so!

115 Doulton & Co
1875; murals
Lloyds Bank, F
Street. The ent
ce hall is cove
with elabor
faience tiles. In
banking-hall pan
illustrate charac
in Elizabeth
drama and fl
designs. Heral
devices were u
in the panels co
memorating
buildings on
same site. Llo
Bank, London.

Collecting tiles

There has been a deliberate attempt in this book to avoid qualitative judgements—it is felt that this is a field where individual preference is of far greater value than a rather false indication as to what is a 'good tile' and what the collector should consider important. The antique business is booming at the moment and tiles are becoming increasingly popular. A single Wedgwood tile from the *Midsummer Night's Dream* series or the months of the year may be as much as £15 ($30). There is nothing to justify such a high price. The name Minton still has some of its old magic and many regard that as a justification for charging £6-£8 ($15) a piece; 'Ah yes, Sir, but it's Minton!' should be a sufficient deterrent for any buyer. There are so many tiles, named and unnamed, that the collector should not be worried by the artificial prices that are sometimes asked for. Tiles can be bought for a couple of pounds and unless you are keen to obtain a set of a particular kind it need never be an expensive hobby.*

The first thing, then, is—find a tile that you like. After that, the following notes might help some people to make more sense of their collection, by learning more about it.

Hints for collectors

There are considerable difficulties in identifying tiles. Many of the mass-produced tiles give little or no information as to their origin: several firms were only decorators and did not bother to sign their work; many made biscuit for other companies as well as their own; some of the less reputable firms copied designs and even if a tile appears to be part of a set there is no guarantee that it was made by a particular firm, unless it is specifically so stated; furthermore it is easy to guess at the stock problems involved for a large manufacturer and it is quite likely that the wrong biscuit was sometimes used by mistake.

The back of a tile may be more informative than the front. See if there are any marks which might indicate a date or manufacturer. Any mark impressed or moulded into the tile may give a clue as to who made the biscuit, a further printed or painted mark may suggest that it was decorated by a different company. Quite often there are no marks at all. Catalogues of the period may be useful.

The next step is to discover how the tile was made. Was it dust-pressed or moulded from plastic clay? Dust-pressed tiles nearly always have a characteristic key back with a pattern of bars or squares. As a

---

* Prices have risen since 1972. It was suggested then that building sites offered a good hunting ground for cheap tiles, but builders now know their value and fewer houses are now being demolished. Indeed many collectors complain that they have difficulty in finding tiles at all. Increased demand results in an increased price. De Morgan tiles can cost anything from £15-50 ($30-100) and hand-painted panels may cost upwards of £100 ($200). Generally prices reflect quality, although a simple transfer print may be a better buy at £2 ($4) than a more complex and more expensive tile.

means of identifying the manufacturer, however, the pattern of the key back has been found unreliable—not only because unmarked biscuit may have been used but also because two different firms may have used moulding plates of the same design.

The process(es) employed in decorating the tile can call for real detective work. It is usually possible to tell where a transfer print has been used, and look for minor irregularities in the outline of the colouring to see whether it was filled in by hand or printed by the lithographic process. Feel the surface of the tile: overglaze painting can often be detected in this way. If the tile has an iridescent glaze or is lustre, take it to the light and see how well the colours are reflected. If the tile is part of a set, it is often possible to discover more by comparing the different tiles, the colours may be stronger in some cases or the image clearer and the outline more accurately followed. If it is hand-painted that may not be such a great virtue; notice how well it was done, as well as how it was done.

It may be interesting and informative to know how and where the tiles were used. A set of five or six could have been inserted into the back of a wash-stand. Traces of soot or stove-black obviously indicate that the tile came from a fireplace. Quite a lot of tiles were sold as teapot stands and may have the original wooden or metal frame. Others which have been used on the wall will probably have traces of cement, mortar or plaster.

Dating

In some cases an accurate date can be determined from the printed or impressed design-registration number on the back of the tile. From 1842–83 a diamond-shaped figure gave coded information as to when the design was registered at the Patent Office in London. These marks are not particularly common on tiles and the lack of such a stamp does not mean that the tile post-dates that period. Some floor tiles were marked in this way but comparatively few wall tiles were produced before 1870.

The stamp gives five pieces of information. In a circle at the top is the class number: in the case of tiles this is 'IV'. In the four corners of the diamond are letters and numbers that code the year, month and day and the parcel number of that batch of tiles.

(14 November 1881)

From 1842-67 the year letter was at the top, below the class number. From 1868–83 the year letter was on the right hand side.

The letters were not used in sequence and this table gives the date codes:

1842–67		1868–83	
A = 1845	N = 1864	A = 1871	V = 1876
B = 1858	O = 1862	C = 1870	W = 1878
C = 1844	P = 1851	D = 1878	X = 1868
D = 1852	Q = 1866	E = 1881	Y = 1879
E = 1855	R = 1861	F = 1873	
F = 1847	S = 1849	H = 1869	
G = 1863	T = 1867	I = 1872	
H = 1843	U = 1848	J = 1880	
I = 1846	V = 1850	K = 1883	
J = 1854	W = 1865	L = 1882	
K = 1857	X = 1842	P = 1877	
L = 1856	Y = 1853	S = 1875	
M = 1859	Z = 1860	U = 1874	

The months for both periods:

A = December	E = May	K = November
B = October	G = February	M = June
C/O = January	H = April	R = August
D = September	I = July	W = March

From 1884 onwards, consecutive numbers were used. These are rather more common, but again, relatively few pieces were marked. For stock purposes the manufacturers had their own coding system and these can often be seen stamped on to the back of a tile as an odd letter or series of numbers. In some cases a number was painted on to the biscuit during decoration. This could be taken to be either a stock number or the number of the tile as it was to be set in a panel, or possibly the factory number of the artist. In any case, it is difficult to draw any information from it.

The official registration numbers are nearly always prefixed by 'Rd' or 'Rd No.'. The year of the tile is shown in the sequence below. But it should be remembered that this date applies only to the registration of the design: it could have been in production before that date but not registered and certainly may bear a registration number that does not equate with the year of manufacture of that particular tile. However the dates can be used as an approximate guide.

Rd No.			
1—1884	163767—1891	311658—1898	*447000—1905
19754—1885	185713—1892	331707—1899	*471000—1906
40480—1886	205240—1893	351202—1900	*494000—1907
64520—1887	224720—1894	368154—1901	*519000—1908
90483—1888	246975—1895	*385500—1902	*550000—1909
116648—1889	268392—1896	*402500—1903	
141273—1890	291241—1897	*420000—1904	

* approximate only.

155

Other clues to the date can be derived from the following:

Any form of trade-mark is likely to mean that the tile was made subsequent to the Trade Marks Act of 1862.

Any form of Limited, Ltd., Ld., is certainly post 1860 and was not general in any field of ceramics prior to the 1880s.

A diamond shaped mark means that the tile was made before 1884.

Rd. No. means that the tile is post 1884. Any numbers over 360000 were made after the turn of the century.

The word 'ENGLAND' will only be found on tiles after 1891 (it was introduced to comply with America's McKinley Tariff Act). But the omission of England may simply mean that the tile was not made for export.

'MADE IN ENGLAND' always denotes a twentieth-century tile.

Another dating system was a mark such as $\frac{1}{75}$ which stands for January 1875. ($\frac{5}{16}$ would correspond to May 1916). These may been seen on Copeland tiles—the month given by letters 'O' for October, etc.

Some tiles carry a mark such as 'I . .'. The number denotes the year (1901) and the number of dots shows the seasonal quarter (two dots— April, May, June).

British tile manufacturers and their marks

The following list of manufacturers is arranged alphabetically. For the most part, only nineteenth-century firms are included, although a few of the more important companies that were established soon after 1900 are also listed. Only verified information is given and where the facts cannot be easily substantiated, a reference is appended. Dates given apply to tile production only.

1 Adams & Bromley
c. 1895

Ref: Tile Association records.
Tile decorators only.

Trade
Vine
Mark

Made By
Adams & Cartlidge Ltd
Vine St Hanley

2 Adams & Cartlidge Ltd
Vine Street, Hanley,
Staffordshire
c. 1900

Information uncertain, but may well have been successors to Sherwin & Cotton of the same address.

Ap. Co

Ap. Co
Poole
Patent

Architectural
Pottery Company
Poole Dorset

3 Architectural Pottery
Co.†
Poole,
Dorset
1854–95

After 1861 the firm was run by T. & F. Sanders. A full range of encaustic tiles, faience and terracotta was made. Taken over by Carter & Co. in 1895. The firm supplied biscuit for William De Morgan.

156

4 Art Tileries
Stourbridge,
Worcestershire
c. 1895

Ref: Tile Association records. Tile decorators only. This may have been the firm of Gibbons, Hinton & Co. from the same town (36).

5 J. H. Barrett & Co.
Boothen Works,
Stoke-on-Trent,
Staffordshire
c. 1895

Little is known about the firm, but in 1897 they were taken to court by Godwin & Hewitt over the theft of a design. This firm was also the first pottery to install a tunnel kiln for tiles in 1913.

6 Barry & Co.
Woodville Tile Works,
Burton-on-Trent,
Staffordshire
c. 1880

Ref: Jewitt.

7 Bates Dewsberry & Co.
Mayer Street, Hanley,
Staffordshire

Ref: *Pottery Gazette* 1899.

Blashfield	}	impressed
J. M. Blashfield		1840-58
Blashfield	}	impressed
Stamford		1858-75

8 J. M. Blashfield
London
1840–75

Involved in production of encaustic tiles and mosaics, at an early date. He worked with Herbert Minton in some capacity, but the relationship is not clear.

T. & R.B.
T. & R. Boote
T. B. & S.

9 T. & R. Boote Ltd*
Waterloo Pottery Burslem,
Staffordshire
1850–1963

Boote's was established in 1842 and made their 'patent ironstone' and other china ware prior to the production of tiles. They were the patentees of the process of dust-pressing encaustic tiles, 1863. They made large numbers of majolica tiles towards the end of the century, using a trade-mark crest of Greyhound couchant, collared and slipped between two laurel wreaths. It is said that the idea for the crest came from the success of one of Tom Boote's grey-hounds, which won the Waterloo Plate.

T. G. & F. B.

10 T. G. & F. Booth
Church Bank Pottery,
Tunstall, Staffordshire
1883–91

Ref: Godden; Mercantile Directory & Manufacturers Guide 1887, Transfer-printed 'art tiles' were a speciality.

11 Broseley Tileries
Broseley, Shropshire
c. 1890

Ref: Tile Association records. From the same district as the famous firms of Maw's and Craven Dunnill.

12 Robert Brown & Co.
Ferguslie Fireclay Works,
Paisley, Scotland
1873–1933

Ref: Tile Association records; Godden.

13 Brown Westhead Moore
& Co.
Stoke-on-Trent,
Staffordshire
c. 1885

Ref: Mercantile Directory and Manufacturers Guide 1887.

Burmantofts
Faience

14 Burmantoft's
Leeds
1882–1904

Owned by Wilcock & Co. Specialized in architectural faience work. W. J. Neatby worked with the firm until 1890. The company later became Leeds Fireclay.

15 Camm Bros.
Smethwick,
Staffordshire
c. 1870–80

Ref: Jewitt.
Hand-painted tiles on commission.

The Campbell
Brick & Tile Co.
Stoke upon Trent

16 Campbell Brick &
Tile Co.*
Stoke-on-Trent,
Staffordshire
1875—

Colin Minton Campbell was the proprietor and Robert Minton Taylor the manager. The company was formed after a court case with Minton, Hollins's and was to have been called 'Minton Brick & Tile Co.'. They quickly took a commanding position in the market, producing a full range of tiles. Later Campbell Tile Co. Ltd.

Carter
Poole

Carter & Co.
Carter Poole

17 Carter & Co. Ltd†
Poole, Dorset
1873—

Specializing in ceramic murals, this firm had a considerable reputation in the 1880s. In 1895 they bought out their local rivals, the Architectural Pottery(3).

18 Carter Johnson & Co.
Worcester
c. 1895

Ref: Tile Association records.

19 C✳B

No information. Possibly Camm Bros (15).

Chamberlains

Chamberlains
Worcester

20 Chamberlain & Co.
Worcester
1836–48

Fleming St John, G. Barr were one of the first firms to make encaustic tiles. In 1840 they amalgamated with Chamberlain & Co., their local rivals. Tile production stopped in 1848 and the stock was bought by Maw's (52) in 1850.

Copeland & Garrett
(1835-47)

W. T. Copeland
(1847-67)

W. T. Copeland & Sons
(1867-   )

Copelands

Copeland

Fresco

21 W. T. Copeland & Sons
Spode Works,
Stoke-on-Trent,
Staffordshire
1836—c. 1900

'One of the early firms to succeed with encaustic tiles' (Jewitt). They made many 'art tiles' in the seventies and eighties using a transfer-printed outline and hand-painted colours. Plastic clay tiles have a characteristic key-back which was done by drawing a comb through the clay in two directions. Some tiles were also dust-pressed.

22 W. & E. Corn*
Top Bridge Works,
Longport, Staffordshire
1891–1903

The company was established in 1837 producing earthenware; they started tiles in the 1890s (Tile Association members 1894). Later became Henry-Richards Tile Co.(61); the name was taken from the second Christian names of the two Corn brothers.

23 C.O.V.

no information

24 J. M. Craig
Kilmarnock
Scotland
c. 1870–1900

Ref: Jewitt; Tile Association records.

25 Craven Dunnill & Co.
Jackfield,
Shropshire
1872–1951

Craven Dunill
& Co. Jackfield
Salop

Jackfield

One of the Ironbridge Gorge firms. The oldest works in Shropshire; formerly Hargreaves & Craven and on the same site as used by Peter Stephan, who attempted to make encaustic tiles c. 1800 (marked with anchor and cable) but these were rare even in 1880.

C P P Co.

**26 Crystal Porcelain
Pottery Co. Ltd**
Elder Road, Cobridge,
Staffordshire Potteries
c. 1890

Ref: Godden; Tile Association records. The company was possibly the predecessor of H. & R. Johnson(43), established 1901.

27 Decorative Art Tile Co.
Hanley, Staffordshire
c. 1885–1900

Ref: Tile Association records.
Decorators only.

Della Robbia

28 Della Robbia Co. Ltd
Birkenhead, Cheshire
1894–1901

The firm made more plaques than tiles. Hand-made and -painted; they did reproductions of some of Burne-Jones's designs. Established by Harold Rathbone, a former pupil of Madox Brown. Very distinctive ware, sculpted in relief and coloured with pale greens and yellows.

29 William De Morgan
1872–1907

His early tiles were unmarked and decorated on blanks by other potters, but still distinctive in style. Only a selection of marks illustrated (for full details see *William De Morgan* by William Gaunt and M. D. E. Clayton-Stamm).

30 Walter Pen Dennis
Ruabon, Wales
1891–1901

Ref: Godden.

Doulton & Co. Ltd
Doulton Burslem
Lambeth Faience

31 Doulton & Co. Ltd
Lambeth, London
1870—c. 1915

For the most part they only decorated tiles, but produced much faience work. They used Craven Dunnill tiles with overprinted mark. Some tiles marked as 'Doulton Burslem' were decorated in Staffordshire. See Pinder Bourne(58).

J. C. Edwards
Penybont
Ruabon

32 J. C. Edwards
Trefynant Works,
Ruabon, Wales
c. 1870–1900

The firm made architectural ornaments of many kinds, including tiles.

33 W. England & Sons

No information.

34 T. Forester & Sons
c. 1895

Ref: Tile Association records.
A short-lived firm of decorators.

35 Gateshead Art Pottery

Ref: *Pottery Gazette* 1899.

36 Gibbons, Hinton & Co.
Stourbridge, Worcestershire
1883–c. 1950

Ref: *Pottery Gazette* 1899.

G & HH

G. & H. H.

37 Godwin & Hewitt
Victoria Tile Works,
Hereford
1889–1910

Ref: Godden; Tile Association records.

W. Godwin
Lugwardine

38 W. Godwin
Lugwardine, Hereford
1861—

One of the earlier firms to make floor tiles: Eastlake commends them.

39 J. Hamblett
West Bromwich,
Staffordshire
c. 1890

Ref: Tile Association records.

40 Hawes & Co.
London
c. 1890

Ref: *Building News* vol. 47. The firm is criticized for attempting imitation encaustic tiles with transfer pattern under thick glaze—a technique that was later used by many other manufacturers.

41 Hopkins

Ref: *Pottery Gazette* 1899.

42 W. P. Jervis
Stoke-on-Trent,
Staffordshire

Decorators only. Probably limited production in the eighties.

43 H. & R. Johnson Ltd*
Crystal Tile Works,
Cobridge, Staffordshire
1901—

Although a late-comer to the industry, this company now dominates all others.

44 Jeffrey William
Johnston & Son

Ref: *Pottery Gazette* 1899.

L. & B.

45 Lee & Boulton

Ref: *Pottery Gazette* 1899.

46 Leeds Art Pottery &
Tile Co.

Ref: *Pottery Gazette* 1899.

47 L.T.

No information.

48 L. & D.

No information.

Malkin Edge & Co.
M. E. & Co.

49 Malkin Edge & Co.*
Burslem, Staffordshire
1866—

An offshoot of Cork, Edge & Malkin. Prolific but mostly for the popular market. Few tiles carry a trade-mark.

M. B.

50 Mansfield Bros Ltd
Art Pottery Works,
Woodville
c. 1890

Ref: Tile Association records.
Also of Church Gresley, Burton on Trent. Probably only decorators.

51 Marsden Tiles*
c. 1895–1918

Ref: Tile Association records.

Maw

Maw & Co.
Benthall Works
Broseley
Salop

Maw & Co.
Benthall Works
Jackfield
Salop

Floriat Salopia

52 Maw & Co.*
Benthall Works,
Broseley/Jackfield,
Shropshire
1850–1967

In the last decades of the century, Maw's were the largest tile manufacturers in the world. In 1883 they moved to new premises covering five acres, in Jackfield, with every convenience in services and layout. A complete range of tiles and panels were produced, their imitation of old Persian tiles being particularly well thought of.

Minton's
China Works
Stoke on Trent

Minton's

53 Minton's China Works
Stoke-on-Trent,
Staffordshire
1830–1918

A detailed history of Minton's, being a name which has caused some confusion, is given in the Appendix. Under this name Colin Campbell's firm produced decorative wall tiles of every kind but not floor tiles. The firm specialized in sets of transfer-printed tiles: Fables (*x12*); Waverley (*x12*); Tennyson (*x12*); Early English History (*x12*); Thomson's Seasons (*x12*); Shakespeare (*x24*); Old and New Testament (*x24*). Also hand-painted work by Solon and others.

Minton & Co.
Stoke upon Trent

Minton Hollins & Co.
Stoke on Trent

54 Minton, Hollins & Co.*
Stoke-on-Trent,
Staffordshire
1845–1962

Until 1868, as above, Perhaps the best known name in the business and for many years unchallenged as leading manufacturer, making a full range of tiles of every description. Floor tiles marked Minton & Co.

55 Ollivant

Ref: *Pottery Gazette* 1898.

56 Photo Decorated
Tile Co.

Ref: *Pottery Gazette* 1899.

P.

57 Pilkington's Tile &
Pottery Co. Ltd.†
Clifton Junction,
Manchester
1897—

They were latecomers to the industry, but quickly earned a reputation for well designed products. Designs by Walter Crane, Lewis Day, and Voysey. Under the name of Pilkington's & Carter this firm is now a major manufacturer in Britain.

P. B. & Co.

58 Pinder Bourne & Co.
Nile St,
Burslem, Staffordshire
1862–82

Uncertain as to how far the firm was involved with tiles. Purchased by Doulton's for £12,000 in 1876 and used for production of art pottery and tiles.

59 Porcelain Tile Co.
Hanley, Staffordshire
c. 1890

Ref: Tile Association records.

60 Prestage

Ref: *Pottery Gazette* 1899.

61 Richards Tiles*
Pinnox Works,
Tunstall, Staffordshire
1903—

See W. & E. Corn(22). During the twentieth century this firm grew to a position of eminence in the industry.

Sherwin & Cotton
Sherwin's Patent Lock

62 Sherwin & Cotton*
Vine St,
Hanley, Staffordshire
1877–1911

Prolific manufacturers of majolica tiles, and those made by a photographic process.

63 Shrigley & Hunt
London & Lancaster
c. 1880

Ref: Catalogue Victoria & Albert Museum. Designers only.

T. A. S. Ltd
T. A. Simpson
Hanley

64 T. A. Simpson & Co. Ltd
Furlong Tile Works,
Burslem, Staffordshire
c. 1890–1969

Ref: Tile Association records.

65 W. B. Simpson
& Sons Ltd
St Martin's Lane,
London
1870–*c.* 1900

Decorators only. The firm was responsible for many ceramic panels, as well as a few single tiles. They used biscuit made by Minton's and Maw's, occasionally found with their own trade-mark embossed on the back.

66 Skey & Co.
c. 1890

Ref: Tile Association records.

E. Smith
Coalville

67 E. Smith & Co.
Coalville, Leicestershire
c. 1890

Ref: Tile Association records.

68 Smith & Ford
Lincoln Pottery,
Burslem, Staffordshire
1895–98

Ref: Godden; Tile Association records.

69 W. T. H. Smith Ltd
Cable Pottery,
Longport, Staffordshire
1898–1905

Ref: Godden.

	70 Steele & Wood London Road, Stoke upon Trent, Staffordshire 1874–*c.* 1900	Ref: Jewitt; Tile Association records.
	71 Stone & Co.	Ref: *Pottery Gazette* 1898.
	72 Stubbs & Hodgart Longport, Staffordshire *c.* 1890	Ref: Tile Association records. Decorators only.
	73 Sugden Bros.	Ref: *Pottery Gazette* 1898.
	74 C. P. Sutcliffe & Co. Ltd Higher Broughton, Manchester 1885–93	Little known about this firm but it was bought by Maw's in 1893.
	75 Tamar & Coalville	Ref: *Pottery Gazette* 1899.
R. M. T. **F. T. W.** **Robert Minton Taylor** **Tile Works** **Fenton near** **Stoke on Trent**	76 Robert Minton Taylor Tile Works, Fenton, Staffordshire 1869–75	Previously of Minton, Hollins's and later of Campbell Brick and Tile Co. (see Appendix.)
	77 Charles Timmis & Co. Sheaf Works, Longton, Staffordshire *c.* 1895	Ref: Tile Association records. Decorators only, for brief period in 1890s.
	78 J. & W. Wade Burslem, Staffordshire *c.* 1895	Ref: Tile Association records. Decorators only. Later A. J. Wade.
79 T. W. Walker **Patent Encaustic &** **Mosaic Ornamental** **Brick & Tile** **Manufactury** **East Quay Rd, Poole** **Dorset**	79 T. W. Walker East Quay Road, Poole, Dorset, 1861–73	Walker was chief technician at Architectural Pottery, Poole, before starting his own firm specializing in floor tiles. Carter's purchased the company in 1873.
Webb's Worcester **Tiles** **Henry C. Webb** **Worcester**	80 Webb's Worcester Tileries Rainbow Hill, Worcester, 1870–1905	Ref: Jewitt. Established by Henry C. Webb.

Josiah
Wedgwood & Sons
Etruria
Patent
Impressed Tile
Wedgwood

81 Josiah Wedgwood
& Sons Ltd
Etruria,
Staffordshire
c. 1870–1900

Mostly transfer-printed work with sets such as the months of the year; Little Red Riding Hood (x6); Midsummer Night's Dream (x12); Robin Hood (x10). Also many animals and Landseer-like scenes, photographic views of American monuments, and series of sailing ships.

82 Wood & Co.
Stoke-on-Trent,
Staffordshire

Ref: Tile Association records. Decorators only.

83 Wooliscroft & Sons
Hanley, Staffordshire
1880—

Ref: Godden; Tile Association records. The company is still in production.

*H. & R. Johnson-Richards Tiles Ltd (now part of the Norcros Group) was formed in 1968 after the merging of interests between H. & R. Johnson Ltd and Richards Campbell Tiles. Malkin Tiles (Burslem) also joined the new group later in the same year. Interwoven into the structure of this new company are most of the old names of the tile industry: Maw, Minton Hollins, Campbell, Malkin Edge, Sherwin & Cotton, T. & R. Boote. Today the company is one of the largest tile manufacturing groups in the world, with factories on five continents, and an annual turnover approaching £60 million.

†The other major manufacturer in Britain is the Manchester-based firm of Pilkington's & Carter.

American tile manufacturers

1 Alhambra Tile Co., Newport, Kentucky. Established 1892.
2 American Encaustic Tiling Co., Zanesville, Ohio. Established 1875 by Benedict Fischer; Hermann C. Mueller was employed 1886.
3 Beaver Falls Art Tile Co. Ltd, Beaver Falls, Pennsylvania. Established 1887 by F. W. Walker. Isaac Broome was employed for a number of years.
4 Cambridge Art Tile Works, Covington, Kentucky. Established 1887 by the Busse brothers.
5 Ceramic Tile Works, Toledo, Ohio. A short-lived company that failed in 1892.
6 Columbia Encaustic Tile Co., Anderson Indiana. Established 1887 by B. O. Haugh and George Lilly.
7 Enfield Pottery & Tile Works, Enfield, Pennsylvania. Established 1906.
8 Grueby Faience Co., Boston, Massachusetts. Established 1891 by William H. Grueby.

Production started with briquettes for the linings of fireplaces. In 1909 Grueby set up the Hartford Faience Co. after his first company had failed two years earlier.

9 Hamilton Tile Works, Hamilton, Ohio.
Several firms were set up, only to fail a few years later and insufficient information prevents more details.

10 Hartford Faience Co. Established by W. H. Grueby in 1909.

11 Hyzer & Lewellen, Philadelphia.
One of the few firms in production before 1870.

12 International Tile Co., Brooklyn, New York. Established c. 1882 and financed from England.
The equipment and many of the workers were brought over too, probably from Maw's of Jackfield. In 1888 the company was taken over by the New York Vitrified Tileworks.

13 Kirkham Art Tiles, Barberton, Ohio.
Run only for a few years and closed in 1895. Kirkham was instrumental in starting the Providential Tile Co.

14 J. & J. G. Low, Chelsea, Massachusetts. Established 1877 by John G. Low.
One of the earliest American art tile companies, but they went out of business in about 1893. Arthur Osborne was the chief modeller up to that time.

15 Matawan Tile Co., Matawan, New Jersey.
The company started making tiles on a small scale in 1898, but closed in 1902. After various changes in name, the old firm was re-established and continued production.

16 Maywood Art Tile Co., Maywood, New Jersey.
This factory was originally used as a foundry and machine shop for making iron stoves. In 1891 it was reorganized for tile production which continued until the works were closed in 1905.

17 McKeesport Tile Co., Pennsylvania. Failed 1895.

18 Menlo Park Ceramics Works, Menlo Park, New Jersey.

19 Moravian Pottery and Tile Works, Doylestown, Pennsylvania. Established 1899 by Henry C. Mercer.

20 Mosaic Tile Co., Zanesville, Ohio. Established 1895 by Herman C. Mueller and Karl Langenback, both from the American Encaustic Tiling Co.
After slow and hazardous early years, the company grew into a pre-eminent position in the trade.

21 Mueller Mosaic Co., Trenton, New Jersey. Established 1908 by Herman Mueller after he left the Mosaic Tile Co. in 1903.

22 New Jersey Mosaic Tile Co., Matawan, New Jersey.

23 New York Vitrified Tileworks, Brooklyn, New York. Established 1888.

24 Old Bridge Enamelled Brick & Tile Co., Old Bridge, New Jersey. Established c. 1890 by W. E. Rivers.

25 C. Pardee Works, Perth Amboy, New Jersey. Established 1894 by Calvin Pardee.

26 Park Porcelain Works, West Philadelphia. Established 1884.

27 Penn Tile Works Co., Aspers, Adams County, Pennsylvania. Established 1894 for the manufacture of encaustic floor tiles.

28 Providential Tile Works, Trenton, New Jersey. Established 1891 by Kirkham, Robinson and Whitehead.
The firm produced no floor tiles and claimed to be the first American company to make decorated tiles, under the direction of Scott Callowhill.

29 Robertson Art Tile Co., Morrisville, Pennsylvania. Established 1890 by George W. Robertson, his son Hugh C. Robertson being a modeller.
About 1893 the family withdrew from the firm, although it retained the same name and in the following years attracted many of the most talented ceramic artists in the country.

30 Rookwood Pottery Co., Mount Adams, Cincinnati, Ohio.
One of America's most celebrated pottery companies, from 1880 they made a number of finely painted art tiles.

31 South Amboy Tile Co., New Jersey. Failed by 1900.

32 Star Encaustic Co., Pittsburgh, Pennsylvania. Established 1876. Samuel Keyes was the first American successfully to make encaustic tiles, beginning in 1867. A company was later formed, but by 1905 it was liquidated.

33 H. L. Swift, Riverside Indiana.

34 Tarrytown Tile Co., New York. Failed by 1900.

35 Trent Tile Co., Trenton, New Jersey. Established 1882.
By 1910 it was one of the outstanding tile companies in America but two years later it was in the hands of the receiver.

36 Wheatley Pottery Co., Cincinnati, Ohio. Established 1879 by Tom Wheatley.
The company was involved in the production of architectural ceramics and faience.

37 United States Encaustic Tile Works, Indianapolis, Indiana. Established 1877 by William Harrison.
The company failed ten years later but was reconstituted and continued production until 1932.

38 United States Pottery, Bennington.

Appendix:
Who were the real Mintons?

Hollins v Campbell and Taylor: May 1875.

This dispute, which dealt with the right to use the name Minton on tiles, is a curious piece of history. Parts of the judgement, given by Vice-Chancellor Malins, are quoted here:

> This case is one of very great importance, affecting the fair dealings between persons who have been in partnership; and after all I have heard I should not have contemplated that a gentleman in the position of Mr Campbell [High Sheriff and local member of Parliament] would have thought it worth his while to raise such a contest against his late partner as he has done in this case. The facts of the case are not very complicated. The name 'Minton' is well known in all parts of the civilized world, and the products that pass into the market under that name are invariably admired. The business, it appears, was originally established by Mr Herbert Minton, who died in 1858. In 1841, the plaintiff, Mr Hollins, and the late Mr Herbert Minton were in partnership in the china business, which has become so celebrated, and about the year 1843 [c. 1830, in fact], they added to the china business the manufacture of tiles, called encaustic tiles, which have now become of very great use for application in public buildings and private houses. In 1849, Mr Minton and Mr Hollins took the defendant, Mr Campbell, into partnership with them in the china business and in the tile business. In 1859 (Mr Minton having died in 1858), Mr Hollins and Mr Campbell entered into a new arrangement, and by articles of partnership of the 11th of August, 1859, they made a distinction between the two businesses, it being provided that the style of the co-partnership should, as to the general trade of manufacturers of china and earthenware be 'Herbert Minton & Co.', and as to the particular trade of manufacturers of tiles and mosaic pavements be 'Minton, Hollins & Co.'. So matters continued until 1863, and then a new partnership is formed as to the tile business, into which Mr Taylor is introduced as a member, but the china business was continued, in which he was not a partner. So matters continued until 1868, when Mr Taylor goes out of the business, and there is a partition of the business—I say deliberately, a partition of the business—made between Mr Hollins and Mr Campbell. It was an arrangement of a very fair character; the parties well understood what they were about; and, as I read the arrangement, it was this: 'Mr Campbell takes the exclusive right to the china business. Mr Hollins has the exclusive right to the tile business.' The parties

were trading under the name which did not belong to either of them, and if they had simply dissolved the partnership and made no provision, it is perfectly clear that as to the china or tiles, or anything else, each of them could have had a perfect right to continue to use the name 'Minton' as the firm under which he traded. It was very proper under these circumstances that in dissolving a partnership of this magnitude some arrangement should be made, and it was agreed that Mr Campbell should take the greater business, the china business and that Mr Hollins should take the smaller business, the tile business. Now if that was the arrangement . . . could anything be more fair and proper than that each of them should have the use of the name 'Minton', but that each of them should use the name as applicable only to his own particular portion of the business? . . . I take it to be perfectly clear that the intention of the parties was that the tile business was to be taken by Mr Hollins and the china business by Mr Campbell, and accordingly it was an undisputed fact that from that day (the 12th August 1868) down to this very day, Mr Campbell has had the whole, sole and uninterrupted interest in the china business. On the other hand, up to a very recent period, it is equally clear that Mr Hollins has had the entire and uninterrupted use of the business and profits of the tile business, as far as Mr Campbell is concerned. Other persons have attempted to interrupt it, but not Mr Campbell, although I am sorry to find the attempted interruption was, to a certain degree, supported by Mr Campbell, when the matter was before me in 1871. [It was at this time that Hollins sought an injunction against Taylor, who was trading tiles under the name of R. Minton Taylor: see below.] Up to a recent time, namely the issue of the advertisements on the third of April last, which I shall have a word to say about presently, that was the position of the parties. . . . I take it that the meaning of the arrangement was that Mr Hollins was to have the use of the name 'Minton' as it had up to that time been used; and it is in evidence that for between twenty and thirty years [since 1845], in Staffordshire the business was carried on under the firm of 'Minton Hollins & Co.', and in Conduit Street, London, for more than twenty years, under the style of 'Minton & Co.'. Mr Hollins is, in my opinion, entitled to the use of 'Minton & Co.', which has heretofore been used in London, and he is bound to carry on the business in Staffordshire as it was carried on before this time under the firm of 'Minton, Hollins & Co.'. Of course the great charm in such a case is (whether 'Minton & Co.' only, or 'Minton, Hollins & Co.') the use of the word 'Minton', to which so much celebrity is attached, and from that celebrity so much profit is expected to be derived. Therefore my opinion is perfectly clear that Mr Hollins has acquired the exclusive right to the use of the words 'Minton, Hollins & Co.' as regards to the business in Staffordshire, and to that name of the firm 'Minton & Co.', as it has been for more than twenty years used in London. Now it seemed to be the opinion of Mr Campbell, for he acted upon it for many years. . . . Now comes the curious part of this case. In

1869, Mr Taylor, who had been in partnership with Mr Hollins and Mr Campbell in the tile business, and had gone out of the firm in 1868, set up a business of his own, in partnership with Mr Challinor, at Fenton, which is adjoining Stoke-upon-Trent. The great charm in this case is the use of the word 'Minton' and he therefore began business under the name of 'R. Minton Taylor & Co.'. Now as to R. Minton Taylor and Co., many persons who knew Mr Taylor would know that it meant Robert Minton Taylor and his partners, if he had any, but persons who did not know Mr Taylor would unhesitatingly read this as the firm of 'Robert Minton' as one person, 'Taylor' as another person and '& Co.' as other persons; and the use of the name 'Minton' was therefore an infringement of Mr Hollins's rights. Mr Hollins then filed his bill in 1869 and set up and established against Mr Taylor that he was entitled to the exclusive use of the name 'Minton' as connected with the [floor] tile business. The claim was disputed, and Mr Taylor was represented by Sir Roundell Palmer and the present Vice-Chancellor Hall—most able counsel—but I think I pressed rather hard upon them. I expressed my opinion pretty plainly that I disapproved of it and I disapprove of it now. I think it was one of those not very handsome tricks of the trade by which the truth was attempted to be concealed—namely it was made to appear that Robert Minton was one person [as opposed to Robert M. Taylor]. Upon the third day the defendants made a submission and each party agreed to pay their own costs, and an undertaking was given that the name Robert Minton Taylor should appear in a distinct line, so that nobody could suppose that it was Mr Minton; that the defendants would not make any tiles stamped with the words 'R. Minton Taylor & Co.' or any tiles stamped with the name 'Minton' in a separate line from the name of Taylor, and not make or sell any encaustic tiles or any tiles ordered or intended to be used for flooring or pavements stamped with the words 'Minton & Co.'. Mr Taylor, therefore, with the knowledge of Mr Campbell, submitted to a very stringent injunction, or an undertaking which could have only have been given on the basis that Mr Hollins had established his exclusive title to the use of the word 'Minton' in connection with the manufacture of [floor] tiles. That having been done, I should have hardly thought that Mr Campbell would have considered it worth his while, having bought up Mr Taylor's business, with this undertaking attached to it, to have issued these advertisements to the public, the issuing of which has led to the institution of this suit. [The advertisements went under the name of 'The Minton Brick & Tile Co.'.] Was it a fair or proper thing, under the circumstances, for Mr Campbell to attempt to avail himself of the services of Mr Taylor, and by the assistance of Mr Taylor to do that very thing which Mr Taylor himself was prohibited from doing? . . . Mr Campbell has been, in my opinion, entirely in the wrong by purchasing the business of Mr Taylor and announcing to the public that he is commencing a business in floor tiles of every description—a business which he has set up in opposition to his former partner, to whom he had formally, and for a valuable consideration, parted with the tile business and given to him the exclusive right of carrying on that business. Mr Campbell is, in my opinion, entirely wrong in the whole of the dispute and there must therefore be a decree made against him—there must be a perpetual injunction against him from using the name of 'Minton' in connection with the [floor] tile business. The particular form of it may be considered, and he and Mr Taylor must pay the costs of the suit.

Shortly after this, Campbell and Taylor established the 'Campbell Brick & Tile Co.' which was subject to no such restrictions. At Minton's China Works, Campbell continued to make decorated wall tiles (generally known as majolica, rather than tiles), as he had up to this time; these were of a high quality and not aimed at the popular market as were the products of his second firm. Clearly there was considerable personal enmity between these gentlemen which arose, in part, from Hollins's insistence upon Campbell paying for the stock and equipment at Minton's China Works at valuation (said to be somewhere in the region of £30,000). And so, although Campbell got the better of the deal in theory, Hollins, with great acumen, obtained the capital to build a new and modern pottery for tile production. It is interesting that the new factory cost almost exactly £30,000 (see *The Builder* 1869). With the phenomenal expansion of the market in the 1870s, this gave him the happy and undisputed position of being the leading tile manufacturer in the world.

Glossary of terms

Ark—slip ark: a storage tank in the ground containing liquid clay or other materials which were used in the manufacture of the tiles. To prevent the clay from settling it was agitated with paddles.

Bat: a flat slab of refractory clay or plaster.

Biscuit: sometimes *bisque*, it refers to the fired body of the tile, without decoration or glaze. The clay slab was fired at about 1160°C (2120°F)— the highest temperature, which fixed the dimensions and shape of the tile. At this stage the tile feels and looks like a biscuit.

Blunger: a mixing tank where the clay was beaten by paddles to mix it thoroughly with the water—it was then known as slip.

Burnt: a burnt tile is one that has been fired.

Body: the main portion of the tile, excluding the decoration and glaze. The 'body mix' is the composition of clays that makes up this part of the tile; red clay (Staffordshire) gives a red body, fireclays (Shropshire) give a buff (samian) body, ball clay (Dorset), china clay (Cornwall) and flint, together give a white body.

Clay: although a great variety of clays were used, exploiting different properties for different purposes, the main distinction is to be made between 'plastic clay' and 'dust clay'. Plastic clay has a relatively high water content and can be moulded and shaped by hand, rather like plasticine. Dust clay is drier and although a certain moisture is needed to give it cohesion, it can only be moulded to shape by machine. Dust clay is used in mass-production techniques which employ mechanical presses to form the tiles.

Calcination: method employed to make flint easier to grind; when burnt the flint became brittle.

Cranks, stilts, spurs, etc.: refractory devices for supporting or protecting ceramic tiles during the firing process.

Dies, moulds, etc.: metal and plaster of paris dies were used to shape the surface of tiles, either to form an intaglio pattern which would be filled with coloured slip (encaustic tiles), or to shape the surface, as for embossed tiles with relief decoration.

Drab: body made from dirty or unpurified clays.

Dust clay: finely ground and dried clay.

Earthenware: generic name for pottery but usually confined to pottery made with coarse clays fired at a relatively low temperature.

Embossed: relief pattern moulded on the surface of the tile.

Enamels: low temperature colours usually used for onglaze decoration.

Engobe: a slip coating given to change the surface colour of a tile body. Applied to the biscuit prior to underglaze decoration.

Encaustic: this term only refers to floor tiles which have an inlaid pattern in coloured clay. The inlaid section was fused into the body during firing. Encaustic tiles could be made from either plastic or dust clay.

Faience: a general term referring to all kinds of glazed earthenware, but it came to mean architectural ceramics in particular and it is in this sense that the word is used.

Faults: these may occur in firing—at the biscuit stage the tile may be cracked, dunted (completely broken), nipped (a broken edge or corner), bowed (warped and out of shape) or wedged (irregular dimensions because of uneven firing). A glost tile may be kiln dirty (extraneous particles in the glaze) or have pin holes (where an impurity in the body has blown through the glaze and left a hole unhealed); it may have a missed glaze (areas of glaze missing because of bad handling) or a run glaze (uneven placing in the kiln makes the glaze run to one side of the tile). (See plate 55).

Filter press: a series of hollow trays into which slip is pumped; the water is then expelled through cloths, using the pressure of a dead-weight pump. The hollows between the filter cloths fill with plastic clay. Probably not introduced until after 1900.

Firing: always the most critical stage of production. In the 'bottle-ovens' the clay body was heated to a temperature of about 1160°C (2120°F) when it fused to form a stable material. As the temperature rose the clay contracted more and because the temperature was never perfectly even throughout the kiln, the biscuit had to be graded for size. The tiles were also glost fired at about 1020–40°C (1870–1900°F) to fix the colours and decoration as well as the final glaze. Onglaze decoration was fired at a lower temperature, about 750°C (1380°F), just before the glaze began to run.

Five Towns: the Six Towns of the North Staffordshire Potteries have, by tradition, been known as five because Arnold Bennett forgot Fenton. The towns he mentioned were Burslem, Hanley, Longton, Stoke and Tunstall.

Fixing: Portland Cement was patented in 1828 and mixed with sand it was commonly used to fix tiles. Modern adhesives, which are now used almost universally, were not introduced until the 1950s.

Geometric: these tiles were used for floors and were made up of small sections from a six-inch square. The pattern of the design was formed in different shapes and colours, like a mosaic or tesselated pavement.

Glaze: strictly speaking the glaze of a tile is the impervious coating that covers the body. It could be clear or coloured, transparent or opaque. As a more general term it refers to the superficial treatment of a tile which gave it decoration. This could be underglaze (applied to the biscuit or engobe), inglaze (a stain in the glaze, using metal oxides), or onglaze (decoration on the glazed surface of a fired tile).

Glost: glazed (from glossed—shiny).

Grinder: pan-grinder, a device used to grind stains and colours to a fine paste.

Grog: refractory material (usually ground from old and broken saggars) used to make a body stronger and less liable to deformation. Normally the larger the tile, the more grog that was needed.

Ground: the body of the tile as opposed to the decorative part. Used mostly in association with encaustic tiles where the pattern was inlaid, but it may also refer to the body of glazed wall tiles.

Hardening on: a light low-temperature firing for engobes and under-glaze colours. Mostly used to burn off the oil used in colours for transfer printing.

Incised: cut into the surface—sgraffito work.

Inlaid: as Encaustic.

Intaglio: an indented pattern—the opposite to relief.

Key back, lock back: in order to assist fixing, tiles were sometimes given a shaped back. For most tiles this was a pattern of squares, roundels or bars which were moulded into the tile when it was pressed.

Kiln: see Oven.

Lustre: a type of decoration which gives a shiny metallic surface, obtained by firing metallic oxides in a reducing atmosphere. Wood and rotting vegetables were commonly used or coal gas. Mostly copper, silver, gold, etc.

Majolica: the name was derived from the fine pottery made in Majorca between the fifteenth and eighteenth centuries which was coated in white opaque enamels and painted in bright colours. As applied to tiles, the term was used from about 1850 and denotes a transparent or opaque glaze, applied to the body, often with an embossed pattern.

Mass-production: although it is rather a loose term, it is used with reference to the industrial manufacturers who employed mechanical devices to increase output and efficiency in the production of tiles.

Metal oxides: all metals (copper, manganese, iron, cobalt, etc.) were used as oxides. Copper, which gave a green colour when fired, was actually copper oxide.

Mosaic: a floor treatment that used small pieces of different coloured tiles to form a pattern. A guillotine was used to cut the pieces to shape and then they were pasted, face down, on to a full-size pattern. The spaces were then filled with cement and the panels thus formed were fixed in position on site and the pattern paper removed. Late in the century, Maw's developed a dust-pressed tile that gave the effect of mosaic by impressing an irregular outline into the face. Colours were then fired on to the tile and the channels later filled with cement. This represented a considerable economy in the production of standard mosaic pavements.

Oven, bottle-oven: brick built housing into which ware was placed in saggars, for firing. Through a system of flues, from fireboxes in the outside walls, heat was distributed fairly evenly through the internal cavity. This is the same as a kiln, although that word was not commonly used until after the introduction of the tunnel kiln, in about 1913. The ovens were circular at the base and waisted at the top, like bottles.

Patents: government grant of exclusive privilege of making or selling new invention (OED)—the term of a patent was fourteen years which could be extended for another seven years in some cases.

Press: a machine used for making tiles from dust clay which was compacted under pressure in a die box or mould. The early presses were all operated by hand. After 1873, steam-driven presses were introduced into some factories.

Printing, transfer printing, lithography, etc.: an economical way of decorating tiles in large numbers. Several different processes were employed—the most common was to use a transfer tissue which was printed either using a copper plate or by a lithographic process.

Pouncing: a technique employed to assist the reproduction of a design. Charcoal was dusted through pin holes in a paper—the perforations gave an outline of the design to the biscuit underneath.

Quarries: plain, one-colour floor tiles. In Britain, quarries are regarded as coarse products; in America the term refers to fine floor tiles.

Reduce: a chemical term which referred to the process by which oxygen was abstracted from a compound. In the production of lustre, the reducing atmosphere removes the oxygen from copper oxide, leaving a deposit of metal on the tile.

Refractory: specially compounded clays, fired to a high temperature to give them special properties, as for kiln appliances such as saggars. Heat resistant.

Saggar: a rectangular box (in tile making) made of refractory fireclay which protected the tiles from direct heat during the firing. One of the specialized ancillary trades—the base was batted out (the man who made it was known as a saggar maker's bottom knocker), and then a ring of clay was made around this slab.

Setter tile: a perfectly flat surface, on to which tiles were placed for drying and firing, which helped to prevent warping.

Sgraffito: a technique of decoration. The biscuit was coated with slip and the design scratched away to reveal a different coloured clay underneath.

Sifter: a series of meshes which were used to remove impurities from slip.

Slip: a preparation of fluid clay. In liquid form it was used to decorate tiles or coat them with a surface of fine clay. Slip with a thicker consistency was used to fill the intaglio pattern in an encaustic tile made from plastic clay.

Terracotta: sculpted ornament, fired at a relatively low temperature and used in architectural decoration. It was red-brown and had no glaze or coloured pattern.

Tesserae, tessellated: tesserae are single units in a tessellated pavement. Strictly speaking the term refers to mosaic but it was often applied to geometric tiles or any floor surface composed of several small units. Archaic, mosaic is the word now used.

Tile: distinction must be made between floor tiles (encaustic, geometric, quarry) and wall tiles (decorated, embossed, majolica, printed, etc.). A tile is not usually more than nine inches square although larger pieces were made particularly in America and are here referred to as panels or plaques.

Vitrified: non-porous, will not absorb moisture.

Sources and notes

1   E. Dobson *On Bricks and Tiles*, nd.
2   *The Builder*, Vol. 31, 1873, p. 837
3   William Morris 'The Lesser Arts of Life', in *Lectures in Art*, 1882, p. 195
4   Holbrook Jackson's free quotation of Max Beerbohm's '1870', (*The Yellow Book* Vol. 4 January 1895 pp. 275–83), in *The 1890s*, 1913
5   Society of Arts and Crafts, Boston, *Handicraft*, 1902
6   Ll. Jewitt *Ceramic Art of Great Britain*, Vol. 2, 1878, p. 29
7   ibid p. 195
8   ibid pp. 195ff
9   ibid
10 Stoke-on-Trent City Central Library
11 Jewitt, op cit. Vol. 2, p. 202
12 *Staffordshire Advertiser*, 3 April 1858
13 Benjamin Ferrey *Recollections of A. N. Welby Pugin and his Father*, 1861
14 ibid
15 Charles Eastlake *Hints on Household Taste*, 1867
16 A. Lys Baldry *Modern Mural Decoration*, 1902, p. 122
17 James Francis McCarthy *Great Industries of Great Britain*, Vol. 3, 1875–80, p. 73
18 Lewis F. Day in *Art Journal*, 1895, pp. 343–8
19 William Morris, loc cit.
20 Arnold Bennett *The Death of Simon Fuge*, in 'The Grim Smile of the Five Towns', 1907, p. 216
21 W. J. Furnival *Leadless Decorative Tiles, Faience and Mosaics*, 1904, p. 596
22 Rt. Hon. Joseph Chamberlain *Architect and Reporter*, 15 December 1899
23 C. T. Davis *A Practical Treatise on the Manufacture of Bricks, Tiles and Terracotta*, 1895
24 *Artist and Journal of Home Culture*, Vol. 3, February 1882, p. 51
25 *The Decorator and Furnisher*, 1882
26 Edwin Attlee Barber *Pottery and Porcelain of The United States*, 1909
27 *The Decorator and Furnisher*, 1882
28 J. Milton Robertson—quoted in 'Development of the Tile Industry in the United States', by Everett Townsend, *Bulletin of the American Ceramic Society*, 15 May 1943, p. 129
29 'Some American Tiles', *Century Magazine*, Vol. 23, April 1882
30 'A Trial Balance of Decoration', *Harpers Magazine*, Vol. 64, April 1882
31 Fred H. Wilde, quoted by Everett Townsend, op cit. p. 130

32 ibid p. 134
33 Townsend op cit. p. 132
34 Fred H. Wilde, quoted by Everett Townsend, op cit. p. 148
35 E. Stanley Wires 'Decorative Tiles' in *New England Architect and Builder*, Nos. 14–17, 1960
36 F. P. Slupesky, quoted by Everett Townsend, op cit. p. 128
37 Furnival says that the company was established by Douglas & Hall
38 See *Earthenware and Wall Tile Report*, No. 1, Second Series, Superintendent of Documents, Washington DC, 1940
39 Aymer Vallance *The Art of William Morris*, 1897 p. 79
40 C. R. Ashbee *Memoirs*, Vol. 1, unpublished typescript, 1938. Victoria and Albert Museum Library, p. 19. Quoted by Gillian Naylor, *Arts and Crafts Movement*, 1971, p. 166
41 *The Builder*, Vol. 27, 1869, pp. 411–12
42 Jewitt op cit. new edition, 1883, p. 418
43 Aymer Vallance 'Mr W. J. Neatby and his Work' *The Studio*, 1903, Vol. 29, pp. 113–17
44 P. G. Konody 'Keramischer Wandschmuck und Dekorierte Möbel von W. J. Neatby' in *Kunst und Kunsthandwerk*, 6, 1903, pp. 362–74 Translated by Thomas Stevens
45 ibid
46 ibid
47 The site has recently been redeveloped, and the façade of the old building incorporated into a new office complex
48 *The Builder*, Vol. 31, 1873, p. 973
49 Halsey Ricardo, paper to the Society of Arts in *Journal of the Society of Arts*, 1902

Select bibliography

A Book of the Tile Club. Boston 1886

Aslin, E. *The Aesthetic Movement.* London 1969

Baldry, A. Lys *Modern Mural Decoration.* 1902

Barber, E. A. *Marks of American Potters.* 1904
  Pottery and Porcelain of the United States. 1909

Berendson, Anne *A General History of Tiles,* 1967

Blacker, J. F. *Nineteenth Century Ceramic Art.* 1911

Carter, Owen *On Designing Tiles.* 1893

Davis, C. T. *A Practical Treatise on the Manufacture of Bricks, Tiles
  and Terracotta.* 1895

Dobson, E. *On Bricks and Tiles.* n.d.

Doulton & Co. Ltd *Pictures in Pottery.* 1904

Furnival, W. J. *Leadless Decorative Tiles, Faience and Mosaics.* 1904

Gaunt, W. and M. D. E. Clayton-Stamm *William De Morgan.* London
  and New York 1971

Godden, G. A. *Encyclopedia of British Pottery and Porcelain Marks.*
  1964

Jackson, H. *The 1890s—a Review of Art and Ideas.* 1913

Jewitt, Ll. *Ceramic Art of Great Britain.* 2 vols. 1878

Madsen, S. Tschudi *Art Nouveau.* 1967

Naylor, Gillian *The Arts and Crafts Movement.* London and New York
  1971

'Some American Tiles' *Century Magazine,* New York. April 1882,
  Vol. XXIII

Thomas, John *The Rise of the Staffordshire Potteries.* 1971

Townsend, E. 'Development of the Tile Industry in the United States'
  in the *Bulletin of the American Ceramic Society* Vol. 22 No. 5 May 15,
  1943

Vallance, Aymer *The Art of William Morris.* 1897

Wakefield, Hugh *Victorian Pottery.* 1962

Watkins, Laura Woodside 'Low's Art Tiles' in *Antiques,* May 1944

Watkinson, Raymond *William Morris as Designer.* London 1967

Wedgwood, J. *Staffordshire Pottery.* 1947

Wires, E. Stanley 'Decorative Tiles' in New England *Architect & Builder*
  Nos. 14–17, 1960

Wolverhampton Art Gallery *Victorian Tiles.* Exhibition catalogue, 1978

Index